LAKELAND AVIATION AND AIRFIELDS
IN THE 20TH CENTURY

by
Ken Davies

REGIONAL PUBLICATIONS, FRESHWATER, ISLE OF WIGHT

© 2001 REGIONAL PUBLICATIONS

Printed by
THE WEST ISLAND GROUP
Afton Road, Freshwater, Isle of Wight, PO40 9TT

Published by
REGIONAL PUBLICATIONS
Afton Road, Freshwater, Isle of Wight, PO40 9TT

INTRODUCTION

The combination of Aviation and Lakeland into the 'archive' series has presented two problems. The first is that most of the aviation activities happened in the Second World War period when information of the various units and their purposes were subject to a high degree of security. This resulted in a dearth of photographic material and the author having to rely heavily on such information that was released at the time or very much later. In relation to photographic material, the few that have survived were frequently doctored for censorship purposes and have been published before under captions that are not entirely accurate. Even many of the so-called 'official sources' cannot be relied on to be entirely accurate, and memory has a habit of playing tricks on one.

The greatest problem I have had to face is that my material has been collected over half a century and I have lost touch with many of the sources who originally sent me a particular item or collection. In cases like this, and where I have no idea of the original source, I refer to it as from the author's collection. Should any persons with whom I have lost touch see some item they remember giving to me, please accept my thanks and I would like to think that seeing their gift again gives them as much pleasure as I have had through having it in my collection.

In my books that have relied on past documentation I have had to realise that the passing of time has meant other details have changed over the life of the subject in hand. Mainly because of the above, in this book, where one cannot rely on records, captions have been worded with phrases such as 'similar to' or 'like the one depicted' so as not to disturb the essence of the story. The purpose of this book is to tell of a little-known period of aviation history that took place in an area not generally remembered for air activity.

Something that must be borne in mind with this particular subject is that the very shortage of photographic material available from the early and war years makes quality reproduction difficult. Many of the cuttings are from old magazines and papers and although these do not respond to quality reproduction some have been included because of their subject matter.

Another aspect of the subject is that the very nature of flying and ground activities in the peak war-time years meant that many thousand aircraft of many different types passed through the maintenance and training units based in Lakeland. This makes it impossible to say that any one illustrated would have carried the markings shown in most of the illustrations if or when they were based at the sites mentioned.

To put the picture of Lakeland aviation in some sort of order which will be interesting for the reader, many of the facts are given with a 'then and now' idea in mind and without getting too technical. I hope presenting this little-known part of aviation history in a part of the country where one may least expect it will add to the pleasure and interest of any visit to Lakeland.

Ken Davies, June 2001

EARLY BIRDS AND WATER WINGS

There were flurries of aviation activity in Lakeland before the outbreak of the First World War when the existence of the internal combustion engine was beginning to make itself felt. In the late 1970s some of the older residents claimed to have memories of an airship being built near Barrow in the early part of the century. It is fairly certain that they were remembering the saga of the *Mayfly* which is reasonably recorded, both in records and pictures.

In 1909 the Admiralty asked for tenders for materials for their rigid airship No. 1 which they aimed to have built by Vickers at Barrow in Furness. This seems to be one of the first associations with names that were to become famous in British aviation industry when Short Brothers quoted for the supply of the gas bags, various controls and the outer covering. This airship was to be quite a monster, as the few details of her specification that are a matter of record show. The most impressive figure was that of her gas capacity, which was 706,000 cubic feet. The tail structure consisted of fabric-covered quadruple fins, two horizontal and two vertical, which was different from the more usual triple fins. It was considered that this would reduce the overall horizontal and vertical measurements as well as decreasing the working load on the control surfaces than if they had been of the more common practice of those days.

After two or three tries 'Their Lordships' were convinced that a hull that let the gas out which kept it aloft – and the air in – would sink an airship. They also considered that any ship, be it an Airship or a Warship, was still a ship and therefore should have a strong keel and a proper anchor. They named it 'HMS Mayfly', but it didn't fly, which all got too much for them and they decided to stick to balloons. The result was that the Navy's attempt to fly a rigid airship came to an end before it really got started.

This was all happening in 1911 at Barrow in Furness, in the very early days of aviation development. The Admiralty chose to follow maritime technological developments in which Barrow was able to play a very large part, which included building submarines.

Experiences at Barrow in Furness in the early days of aviation may have been a reason for the Admiralty to chose to develop submarines. Perhaps the determination of the 'Mayfly' to go beneath the waves gave them experience for this!

After a considerable number of acrimonious discussions between the Admiralty, Shorts and Vickers, rigid airship No. 1, now named *Mayfly*, was launched and made its maiden flight in August 1911. It was then that the problems, which were a direct result of the disagreements between Oswald Short and the Admiralty, manifested themselves. The Admiralty had laid down that the outer envelope which had a surface area of 66,000 square feet should be made of water-proofed silk, as were the control surfaces on the rudders and elevators. More importantly, they insisted that the seventeen gas bags be made of laminated cotton and rubber fabric. This was based on their experience with balloons which, as Short pointed out, by the nature of their use were only required to make short flights. The nature of balloon materials which were porous and allowed gas leakage was of little account, but an airship was designed for much longer endurance and such a degree of leakage would be disastrous.

To combat this Short suggested the 'gas bags' be covered with a non porous material such as ox-gut, known in the trade as 'gold beater's skin', which was known to be impermeable to hydrogen. Short was adamant that if the Admiralty got their way the gas would leak. However, in the end they, not for the first time, did get their way – they considered that 'he who pays the piper calls the tune'. They were soon to find out that in this case they were wrong.

The gas bags were installed to the Admiralty's specification and by the time of the launch the leakage was so bad that the gas bags had to be topped up every three or four days. Obviously Short felt vindicated, but it was for him a hollow victory as a week or so later the ship broke her back while being manhandled out of her shed. This was certainly due to the leakage weakening the structure to such an extent that she was quite unmanageable. As a result of this 'Their Lordships' decided that rigid airships were not for them and cancelled all their orders.

An aircraft that originated on the other side of the world, built in Australia, was based on a Farman-type biplane designed and built in 1910 by John R. Duigan. It was well exhibited at a number of events in Australia, but after several accidents Duigan decided it was time he learnt to fly properly. So he packed his bag and his aeroplane and set sail for England. On arrival in the late Summer of 1911 he then set about having the aircraft improved with a series of modifications, some quite radical, by Avro to cure its seeming reluctance to leave earth. A new and more powerful engine was fitted which allowed reasonably predictable flights to be made, although these were confined to straight lines when a passenger was on board. After taking a number of flying lessons, and the aircraft completing four hours in the air under his control without accident, he eventually gained Flying Certificate No. 211 which was good enough for him. Having done what he came for, to learn to fly, once again he packed his bags, put the aircraft up for sale and returned home.

The aircraft was bought, without engine, by the Lakes Flying Company at Windermere, shipped to the lake, and fitted with floats and a more powerful rotary engine which enabled it to serve the company well. A year or so later a pupil pilot was not aware that its glide angle had been altered by a change in the centre of gravity and stalled it a few hundred feet above the lake when attempting to alight on the water. It crashed into the lake, the pilot escaping unhurt although the aircraft was totally destroyed.

Apart from the abortive attempts at airship building and Cdr Schwann's attempts to fly his Avro seaplane at Barrow in Furness, most of the interest in aviation in Lakeland seems to have been centred around Windermere. One of the first names to be noted was that of Oscar Gnosspelius of Hawkshead who had a passion for making flying models. Far from being toys, his models were aimed at the serious purpose of manned flight. He soon found that the lack of large areas of flat land in the middle of Lakeland was an inhibiting factor to his experiments, and he turned his sights on the waters of Windermere.

This must have created quite a bit of interest for any onlookers who may have watched him towing his models at some speed and observing their behaviour. By 1909 he must have been satisfied with the results of his experiments for he commissioned the local firm of Borwick & Sons to build him a full scale 'hydro monoplane'. Further to this, it was his intention to fit it with a 20 h.p. Alvaston engine with the main point being that he believed that from the results of his trials with models his revolutionary design would enable him to make the first man-powered flight from the surface of Windermere.

If Gnosspelius knew it or not isn't recorded, but at the same time a Captain E. H. Wakefield had ordered a Curtis-type biplane from A. V. Roe who had it built under some railway arches at Leyton in north-east London. The plane was taken to Brooklands, presumably to prove it flew, after which Wakefield had it shipped to Windermere where he too sent it to Borwick to have floats fitted.

Captain Wakefield's Avro biplane making the first flight from Windermere in November 1911.

Intentionally or otherwise, this seemed to produce a friendly rivalry between Wakefield and Gnosspelius, who was convinced his monoplane would be the first to fly off the Lake's waters as he was just about ready, as we say these days, 'to go for it'. Came the day and the monoplane was placed on the water, the engine was started and the throttle opened – and that was it! It never left the water, unfortunately crashed and damaged the plane more than somewhat by crumpling the wing and smashing the propeller. Nothing daunted, Gnosspelius ordered its repair – more work for Borwick! He reckoned it was under-powered and said he would try again next year with a 40 h.p. Clerget engine. This he did, and this time the plane is said to have flown well in the hands of Ronald Kemp. This was not soon enough to be the first for it gave Wakefield's Avro built biplane, by then given the name *Waterhen*, the opportunity to make the first flight from Windermere in November 1911. These early flights were followed by others in 1912 and what were quoted as 'locally built aircraft' were probably the *Lakes Waterhen*, *Lakes Seabird* and Gnosspelius's monoplane which was known to have modification work carried out on it by Borwick's and was last heard of flying in 1914.

Capt. Wakefield's Curtis seaplane on its first flight in 1911, passing over the Furness Railways' cargo steamer 'Raven' on Windermere.

    The interesting point about the photograph above is that it is without doubt Wakefield's Curtis on what is quoted by George H. Pattinson in his book 'The Great Age of Steam on Windermere' as flying over the *SS Raven* in 1911 on its first flight. The *Raven* is an interesting vessel in that she was the first and only steam vessel to be a pure cargo boat in service on Windermere, and is still preserved in working order at the Windermere Steamboat Museum for all to see.

One of Wakefield's seaplanes, 'Waterhen', being launched for a flight by a pupil at his Lakes Flying School on Windermere sometime between 1912 and 1914.

Roland Ding, another of Britain's aviation pioneers, was the Lakes Flying School's chief flying instructor and under him the school flourished until 1914 when on the outbreak of the First World War, Kemp, Ding and Gnosspelius left for service in the Forces. The school itself continued as the Northern Aircraft Company, playing a great part in training naval personnel in the new fangled flying techniques.

Barrow was ideally placed for airship operation to provide an anti-submarine patrol over the Irish Sea and indeed some SST types were flown from there. These non-rigid airships were powered by Rolls Royce Hawk engines and this gives us a reason to mention a unique Lakeland aviation connection in an unexpected place. In 1924 Major E. H. Pattinson, father of the founder of the Windermere Steamboat Museum, suggested to a friend that a motor boat club should be formed. This came about in 1926 and Pattinson built his motorboat, the *Gadfly*, and acquired a Rolls Royce Hawk engine from one of the old airships of the SST type to power it.

The boat and the actual engine are still preserved in the museum at Windermere which gives the public a chance to see other aviation exhibits and pictures, including this unique aero engine which is acknowledged as being the oldest working Rolls Royce aero engine in existence.

The SST type of non-rigid airships saw limited service locally, but a Rolls Royce Hawk engine used to power them has one preserved in the Windermere Steamboat Museum, installed in the speedboat 'Gadfly'.

While still on the subject of airships, another saga of Barrow's failure to build a rigid airship came about during the First World War in 1916. Shorts had obtained a contract to build two at Cardington in Bedfordshire. The Duralumin girder work was to be assembled at Walney, near Barrow. The problem arose with this contract because the shed on Walney needed for the assembly was too small for the job and a search had to be made locally to find another. This search failed so it was decided to build a new one 700 feet long at Flookburgh, near the present site of Cark airfield.

As hard as it may seem to believe, this whole project died there and then quite simply because no-one could find enough material to build the shed! Barrow didn't have much luck with rigid airships.

In 1910 the *Daily Mail* offered £10,000 to the winner of a 1,010 mile Round Britain air race. The rules were simple: it had to be flown in five days and there were to be thirteen compulsory control stops, of which Carlisle was one.

There were thirty aircraft entered and ready for the start at Brooklands and it was a pity that out of the thirty only twenty-one actually started – most of the British entries falling by the wayside because of retirements or crashes. This left S. F. Cody in a British aircraft with his *Circuit of Britain* biplane to finish and he came in fourth.

S. F. Cody standing by his 'Circuit of Britain', the only British entry to finish the 1910 Round Britain air race and which came in fourth. One wonders if he flew in his bowler hat? Aviators made their own rules in those days, so he may well have done.

In the years previous to the air race, aviation activity in the Lakeland counties was minimal and to have an event of national importance have a compulsory stop at Carlisle created enough interest locally for the public to come and watch. Bearing in mind that this was before television or even radio, to get any information of this nature meant that one had to rely on the press. With an event of this nature times could not be relied on, so to get even a few dozen spectators was quite an achievement.

From these few snippets of information we do know that Lakeland did join in with the development of aviation and was able to hear a part of the dawn chorus from the early birds.

I suspect that there are still a few local aviation historians who would know the whereabouts in the Carlisle area of the field which the journalists of the day called 'Carlisle Control'. One is forced to wonder what the flasks on the small table contained – refreshment for the pilot perhaps?

If the armband is anything to go by, the elderly gentleman on the left was acting as an official in the race and was probably very proud to be associated with the local connection. Valentine's radial engine looked very substantial for the rather frail looking aircraft to which it was fitted. Perhaps this was a major contribution to his reliability to finish the course third.

Although it cannot be confirmed that the picture above was actually taken at Carlisle Control, it is certain that it is the Bleriot XI of Lieut Jean Conneau who won the race in twenty-two hours and twenty-three minutes, at an average speed of 45 m.p.h.

CARLISLE (KINGSTOWN) 1933–1957

Opened: March 1933 as Carlisle Municipal Airport.
Closed: 1957.
O.S. Map Ref.: NY390595. On A7 two miles N of Carlisle (site now almost completely built over).
Runways: Nil. Grass airfield, but concrete apron and some extra hangers built c.1939.

When the airfield was opened in 1933 it was officially only the second municipal airport in this country to be licensed by the Air Ministry. A few seasonal scheduled services were operated, mainly to the Isle of Man, but private and club flying also provided some minimal aviation activity until the outbreak of the Second World War in 1939.

In 1933 the facilities were of the bare necessity with only one small hanger and one larger one, in addition to a basic admin. building. The unusual feature was the filling station on the adjacent road which had fuel pumps for cars at the front and others for aircraft at the rear.

    The local flying club succumbed to the threat of war, the result of which was that its aircraft were all taken over and the RAF set up elementary training units equipped with DH Tiger Moths and Hawker Harts. The training activities became so intense that an outstation was set up at Burnfoot, a few miles to the north, near Longtown. After the war a number of attempts were made to revitalise the embryo schedules started in the late 1930s, but the heavier aircraft available after the war could not use the field and it was closed in 1957. Before the Council bought Crosby on Eden, a few flights and some private aircraft used Silloth, some twenty or more miles to the west, until Crosby was available as the new municipal airport in 1960.

In the few years between the opening of Kingstown as Carlisle's airport and the outbreak of the Second World War, the aviation activities were confined to club and private aircraft plus some scheduled summer flights to the Isle of Man. There were the odd highlights that don't seem to be recorded except in some obscure book or long forgotten timetable from pre-war airports and aviation centres which no longer exist. The author of this book lived on the Isle of Wight for a number of years and knows that there were at least two airports no longer in existence which offered a service for one year in Spartan Cruiser aircraft from Ryde Airport (now covered by a Tesco supermarket) on the Island to Carlisle.

One is forced to wonder what Kingstown might have been like if it had not been for the war. Those who do remember will know that the fondest memory will be of those aircraft similar to the light, privately-owned De Haviland aircraft such as the Moth variant seen in the picture above.

Two Miles Magisters of No.15 EFTS flying over the Kingstown area c.1940 were typical of the aviation scene as it was influenced by the hostilities, which made an absolute priority for more and more trained pilots.

CARLISLE (KINGSTOWN) c. 1942

By 1942 flying at Kingstown had reached such a density as to become dangerous and a relief landing ground was opened at Burnfoot a few miles to the north. The picture below must have been the view that hundreds of trainee pilots had of Kingstown in the early stages of their training, which did not make their learning easier with the adjacent buildings of 14 MU.

At the outbreak of the Second World War in 1939 the RAF took over Kingstown and prepared it to play its part in the war effort as a base for a number of basic elementary training units. Apart from taking over all the private aircraft that had been based there, Hawker Harts (similar to the one illustrated below), Tiger Moths, Hawker Henrys and many more were to be based there over the next three or four years.

For those who appreciate the lines and similarity between one aircraft and the next from any one company, the drawing above is of a Hart biplane, a type soon to be seen at Kingstown when the RAFVR took over the airfield on the outbreak of the Second World War. She was a forerunner of the legendary Hawker Hurricane which over the next four or five years could have been seen at most Lakeland airfields.

A POST-WAR AIR SERVICE TO CARLISLE

As the Second World War drew to a close, Cumberland County and Carlisle City Councils recognised the certainty that there was going to be a need for replacement of the transport systems worn out in the war years and that advantage should be taken with developments in aviation. They were a bit over the top but it seemed to be a good idea at the time that a brand new international airport would be a good thing to cater for what everybody hoped would be expanding traffic.

BEA started two summer-only round trips and what is now Manx Airlines operated some flights from Nutts Corner to Newcastle via the Isle of Man and Crosby. While this was going on an Isle of Wight firm advertised flights from Cowes to Kingstown and Silloth. These were not scheduled and from the sound of the information available they were probably charter flights very much dependant on weather, as they used aircraft like Austers, Proctors and Spartan Cruisers.

The extract from their rate card below makes interesting reading.

Airfield Served	Distance in Miles	Auster Rate	Time hr min	Proctor Rate	Time hr min
CARLISLE	297	£31 10s 0d (£31.50)	2 58	£47 5s 0d (£47.25)	2 7
SILLOTH	298	£31 12s 0d (£31.60)	2 59	£47 8s 0d (£47.40)	2 8

Any pilot today would be proud of the accurate timing and charging to a few pence as given above. It would seem that this was a product of many hours of good guesswork rather than practical experience.

The Auster Autocrat was the first civil Auster type produced by the company in the immediate post-war years.

What is not obvious from the scale of charges for these flights is whether they were per person or charter of the aircraft for the time. It was probably the latter, as they claimed that all prices were for the return from Cowes airfield and a waiting time of 7s. 6d. (37p) per hour would be made on all journeys over fifty miles. As their flight time works out at an average speed of 115 m.p.h. from Cowes to Silloth, with warning that figures were for still air, this was probably about right when one considers the speed of an Auster! The Proctor was a faster aircraft, so the faster time looks to be OK.

On the question of fares, if our supposition is right the fare works out at about £15 per person. When one considers that the first class rail fare in those days was about £9 per person and the journey took about six hours, that makes an air taxi in the early 1950s a reasonable buy! Taxi, Sir?

HURRICANE AND SPITFIRE

The Hawker Hurricane Mk 1 was the first fighter in the world to have eight machine-guns. During the Battle of Britain in 1940 the Hurricane shot down more enemy aircraft than all other home defence elements combined.

The Supermarine Spitfire Mk Vb – possibly the most famous fighter aircraft in history, and the only Allied fighter to remain continuously in production throughout the 1939-45 war.

SITES OF FURNESS AREA AIRFIELDS

Of the three airfields built during the Second World War, two – Cark and Barrow in Furness – are still active. Millom is now a prison, but a small aviation museum which is open to the public is maintained in an adjacent building which was originally part of the RAF station.

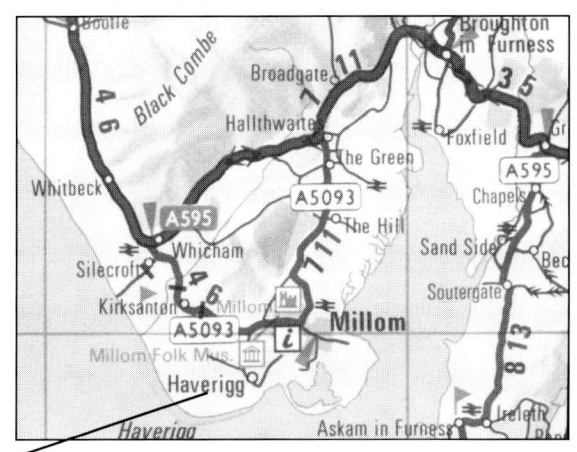

● Site of Millom Aviation Museum and old RAF airfield

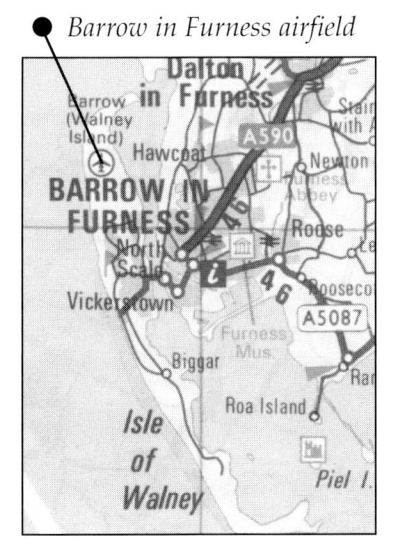

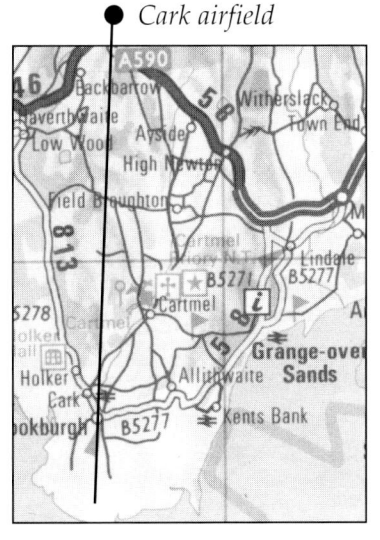

● Barrow in Furness airfield   ● Cark airfield

Barrow and Cark have interesting associations with very early aviation, and are two out of the four airfields in Cumbria that are still active, although not in the same way for which they were envisaged when built. Cark as the North-West Parachute Centre is an entirely recreational airfield, but Barrow is kept open for corporate air traffic in support of the local industry, although a certain amount of private flying and gliding takes place at week-ends.

CARK

Opened: 1941.
Closed: December 1945.
O.S. Map Ref.: SO375745. Two miles SW of Grange over Sands.
Runways: Three when opened.
One, 06/24 1800 x 45 ft, is still serviceable.
Radio: Call sign 'Cark Radio' on 123.45 MHz.

Opened in 1941 by the RAF as a fighter station, Cark was taken over before it was ever used as such by Flying Training Command for the instruction of Air Observers, using an Avro Anson. Other aircraft including Lysanders, Defiants and Henleys were used to provide target-towing aircraft for Millom airfield further up the coast. Towards the end of its active life as a service airfield there were several occasions when personnel took part in mountain rescue activities, especially when the unit which would normally take on that task from Millom was not available, until the MRU moved to Cark from Millom early in 1945.

In September of that year what would now be described as a mini air show was staged as an 'At Home' day and only 3,000 people turned up. This must have been a great disappointment for the organisers. Again, when the station was closed in the December of 1945, nobody really seemed to mourn its loss and it lay disused until taken over for private flying and as a base for parachute training about 1970. Miscellaneous light aircraft now enjoy the use of the field, especially at week-ends when it often gets quite busy, under the control of the Lancashire Parachute Club.

The picture above was taken by one of the Lancashire Parachute Club's free fall photographers from about 12,000 ft directly above the field and clearly shows the layout of Cark, which has not really altered since the day it opened sixty years ago.

CARK AS AN RAF STATION

Cark did yeoman service as an airfield where many pilots were trained in some of the more advanced aspects of flying so they in turn could become instructors. In the first instance Cark itself was not quite complete and those involved in this aspect of training had to commute to and from Millom in an Anson provided for this 'bus service'.

The original of the photograph above has no caption other than 'June 1944, Cark Airfield' scribbled on it. It would seem that it is probably the target-towing flight after promotion to become 650 Squadron.

Cark also hosted 1614 Flight, operating Defiants, Lysanders and Henleys concerned with target-towing for air gunnery training. It would seem that by the time the Flight had become 650 Squadron it was operating Miles Martinet target-towing aircraft and a number of Hurricanes, presumably used to shoot at targets being towed by the Martinets.

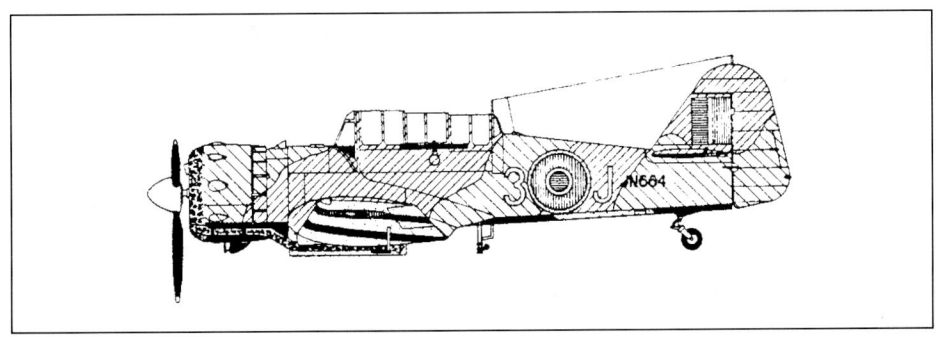

Miles Martinet, a very successful target-towing aircraft, similar to those flown by 650 Squadron at Cark.

Although built as a fighter station, Cark never reached those dizzy heights. Throughout its active life it served the essential function of training air crews in the skills of air gunnery. Another function, less expected but no less essential, took its staff to the 'dizzy heights' that involved mountain rescue. Millom and Cark were both situated on the northern shores of Morecambe Bay, and the Irish Sea beneath the Cumbrian Fells claimed the lives of many airmen and a good few aircraft. For a variety of reasons, primarily to save life, specialised units were officially formed in 1944.

The experience gained in North Wales at the RAF Station at Llandwrog, where the same need had been found due to the high accident rate in Snowdonia, formed the basis of a similar unit to operate in the Lakes and Fells. The record of the first two weeks' operations of the MRU from Cark shows just how great the need for them was.

The above is a rather weather-worn copy of the first operations of a mountain rescue unit at Cark when transferred from Millom in February 1945. Apart from the visits of a number of officials, it logs three operations to crashed aircraft. Because the war was not over at that time, the document was marked secret!

The need for search and rescue services soon became manifest in Cumbria as aviation activity increased rapidly from 1939 onwards, as it was soon found that mountains were not the only hazard for aircraft. Many a plane was forced to ditch into the sea because of engine failure or some other cause. Weather was another prime reason, while others just went missing. In those days helicopters were not so sophisticated as they are today, but never the less Lakeland and its coastline was claiming victims that had to be searched for and rescued.

BARROW IN FURNESS (WALNEY ISLAND)

Opened: October 1941. Still active in 2001 as a privately operated airfield, mainly for local shipbuilding and engineering interests.
Runways: Three, NE/SW 06/24, SE/NW 12/30 and S/N 17/35.
Radio: Call sign 'Walney' on 123.2 MHz.

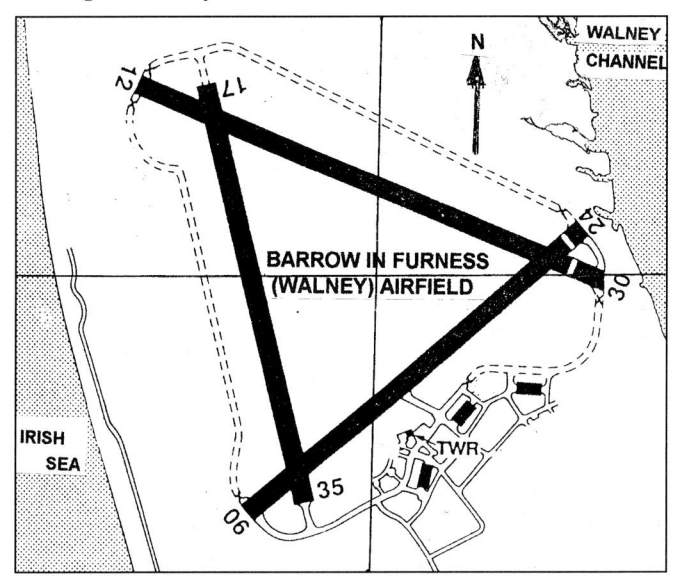

The chart of the modern layout of facilities shows just how little they have altered in six decades.

The Boulton and Paul Defiants were not a great success as fighters as they were more than a little under-powered. However, they were tried out as night fighters and many, some from the Unit shown here, found their way to Barrow where they served a less glamorous but essential task in target-towing and training air gunners.

This picture shows the Barrow in Furness/Walney Island airfield as it looked from about 8,000 feet in 1942. The modern map on the previous page clearly shows that six decades later very little change has had to be made in the original format.

One of the first type of aircraft to come to Barrow, probably just before the view in the photograph at the top of the page was taken in 1942, was a Westland Lysander.

At the time of writing there is only one Lysander still flying, unfortunately not based at Barrow, but the ubiquitous 'Lizzie' will not easily be forgotten. Its unusual wing plan placed it in a class of its own. There was never a problem in its identification and it was commonly said by those who were charged with the job of teaching aircraft identification that all aircraft fell into two classes, 'Lysanders and others'!

A few other units posted detachments to Walney towards the end of the Second World War which included such aircraft types as Vengeances, Oxfords and Spitfires from time to time. Following the end of hostilities, the RAF left the field in 1946 but executive aircraft connected with Vickers Shipbuilding made good use of the facilities, and a limited amount of private aircraft and gliders use it in its civil capacity up to the present day.

In 1984 a small charter company was formed to operate from Barrow with a Piper Aztec aircraft. In the following two years the company started to operate four scheduled flights each week-day between Barrow and Manchester with a number of BN Islanders, under the name of Air Furness. Other schedules were tried between Carlisle, Barrow and the Isle of Man. However, there were a couple of unfortunate incidents when one Islander was written off in an undershoot at Barrow and another had an engine failure and was forced to land on Southport sands.

Although business was continued until 1986, for some reason, probably lack of viable traffic, Air Furness ceased operation. Its licence to fly some routes was taken over by another firm and used on Datapost services. Today the field has some week-end and gliding activity, with the Beechcraft corporate service keeping it open, hopefully for another six decades.

Shipbuilding Engineering operate the Beechcraft Super King Air 300 from their airfield on Walney Island at Barrow, averaging five scheduled flights five days a week on company business. At the time of writing these are probably the only regular scheduled flights from any Cumbrian airfield.

MILLOM

Opened: January 1941.
Closed: September 1946.
O.S. Map Ref.: SD10790.
Runways: Three when built.

Millom opened as a fighter station in 9 Group, and soon became an air gunnery school. The site is now occupied as one of HM Prisons. Many of the old buildings still remain, and one of them has been turned into an aviation museum which is open on Sundays and Bank Holidays with free admission.

Picture taken in 1942 clearly showing the attempts to camouflage the airfield with painted-on hedges. A little counter productive?

The map below shows how familiar the pattern of airfields of six decades ago had become.

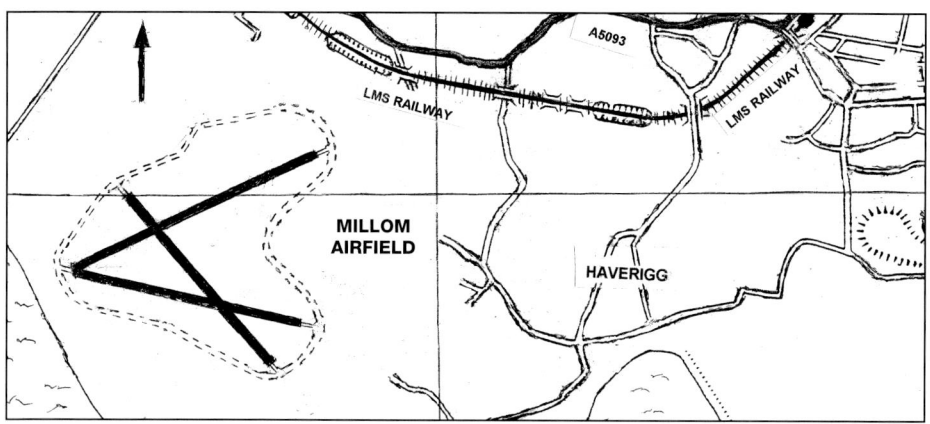

One of the main users of Millom was the School of Air Gunnery and, as with Barrow, Defiants and Miles Martinets played an important part in training activities. The Blackburn Bothas were not so popular – they kept on crashing! These tragic accidents gave rise to the formation of Mountain Rescue teams which have developed into today's sophisticated organisation.

The notorious Blackburn Botha was the sort of aircraft that nobody wanted.

On the face of it the Botha was designed to what seemed a good specification as a reconnaissance torpedo bomber, as was the Bristol Beaufort. Problems were soon discovered when, unlike the Beaufort which had two Bristol 1,130 h.p. engines, the Botha got the short straw with two 930 engines. Together with changes demanded by extra crew and heavier loads, and a tendency to be put into units in mountainous areas like Lakeland, it was soon discovered that the Botha was a very unfriendly plane in such places. It was basically under-powered and when an engine cut out the only direction to go was down. As Lakeland had few alternative landing grounds, the result was that few crews walked away from landings of the forced variety. The only good thing that came from these was that Mountain Rescue units had to be formed, a subject which is dealt with on later pages.

The Miles Martinet was very successful as a target tug (over 1,500 were built), and was seen at Cark, Barrow and Millom between 1942 and 1946.

WINDERMERE

Opened: 1910 and 1942.
Closed: 1944.
Airfield: Windermere.
O.S. Map Ref.: NY390005.
Runways: Lake's waters.

Some early flights were made between 1910 and 1918. In 1942 a factory was set up on the eastern shore of the lake about two miles south of Ambleside to manufacture Short Sunderland Mk III flying boats. Thirty-five of these were made and a few RAF Catalina and other flying boats were brought to the lake for repair and maintenance. When production ceased the factory was dismantled. Wordsworth and others would have been pleased!

TYPICAL EXAMPLES OF AIRCRAFT TYPES THAT HAVE USED FACILITIES OF WINDERMERE AND BARROW IN FURNESS

Rigid airship *Mayfly**		1909
A.V. Roe-built Curtis type biplane (floats installed locally)		c.1911
Hydro Monoplane	Experimental seaplane	c.1912/14
Lakes Waterhen	Seaplane for Lakes Flying Company	c.1912/14
Lakes Seabird	Seaplane for Lakes Flying Company	c.1812/14
Naval airships*	Various between 1912 and 1926	c.1912/26
Short Singapore III		c.1938
Supermarine Stranraer		c.1938
Short Sunderland IIIs (30-plus built on Lakeside)		1942/44
Slingsby Falcon I (waterborne glider)		1943
Short Sandringham		1990
Consolidated Catalina		1996

Those marked * were active in Barrow in Furness area

The consolidated Catalina above was on a flying visit to Windermere in 1996.

FLYING BOATS ON WINDERMERE

In retrospect it was good thinking that, with the pressing need for long range flying boats to combat the submarine menace in the Second World War, the Shorts' connections for over thirty years with the Lakes should once again be turned in that direction. Their factory at Rochester was too near the South-East, making it vulnerable to enemy attack, and in Northern Ireland and Scotland they were already working flat out and other equally pressing demands were being made on them. Hence Windermere.

Two Sunderland III flying boats moored on the lake awaiting flight testing before being allocated to their units for active service.

A temporary factory was set up on the lakeside just south of Ambleside, and the Ministry placed an order for thirty-five Short Sunderland III flying boats to be built in two batches, with the numbers DP176-200 and EJ149-158. It has to be said that the Windermere factory came a little late to make a major contribution to the war, but then as now every little helps, and those that were produced by the lake certainly played their part equal in proportion to the other seven hundred built elsewhere. Two in particular achieved success soon after delivery to their units. No. EJ150 sunk the German submarine U107 only a month or so after entering service, and E387 had only been working with its squadron for a matter of days when it severely damaged and put U387 out of service for good. Sadly they also suffered losses; six were lost in action, four of them losing their crews.

A scene that was repeated many times between 1942 and 1944 when the flying boats built on the lakeside took off for flight testing and joined a squadron for active service.

WINDERMERE'S WATERBORNE GLIDER

Aviation history tells us that right from the early part of the 20th century a number of contributions to man's ability to fly emanated from 'Lakeland'. Of these, the thoughts of one man, Mr T. C. Pattinson, father of the founder of the Windermere Steamboat Museum, have left us with a unique item of aviation history which took off, but never took off. If that sounds like a contradiction of words, read on... It was during the Second World War that it had been suggested clandestine operatives could be landed by gliders which could alight on water where no other place would be suitable. Mr Pattinson of Windermere undertook to convert a Falcon I glider for this purpose in his own workshops, and in 1943 he had it ready for trials which involved towing it off the lake behind a speedboat.

Pattinson's Falcon I glider being prepared for launch onto Windermere for a speedboat to tow it up until it became airborne.

The Falcon flew well, once a few take-off difficulties were overcome.

THE WINDERMERE STEAMBOAT MUSEUM

Experiments with the Falcon glider (*see previous page*) were a great success, although there don't seem to have been any cases where gliders landing on water were ever used on operations. The actual glider is now preserved in the Windermere Steamboat Museum. This unlikely venue, a delight to young and old, houses some unique aviation exhibits and certainly the finest collection of Victorian and Edwardian streamboats – including the *Dolly*, claimed to be the oldest powered vessel in the world.

The waterborne glider which was the subject of a successful trial in the 1940s by the father of the museum's founder. Another rarity is the aero engine below – reputed to be the oldest working Rolls Royce aero engine in the world.

AIRFIELDS IN THE SOLWAY AREA

The site of Silloth is now occupied by commercial interests, Anthorn has a government radio station, and Great Orton has windmill generators along the line of the old main runway and a few minor aviation-related commercial activities using other parts of the old site.

Brayton Park, Wath Head, Hutton-in-the-Forest and Hornby Hall were all returned to agriculture at the end of the Second World War and are now very difficult to locate. Kingstown, Carlisle's old municipal airport, is now almost entirely covered as a built-up area.

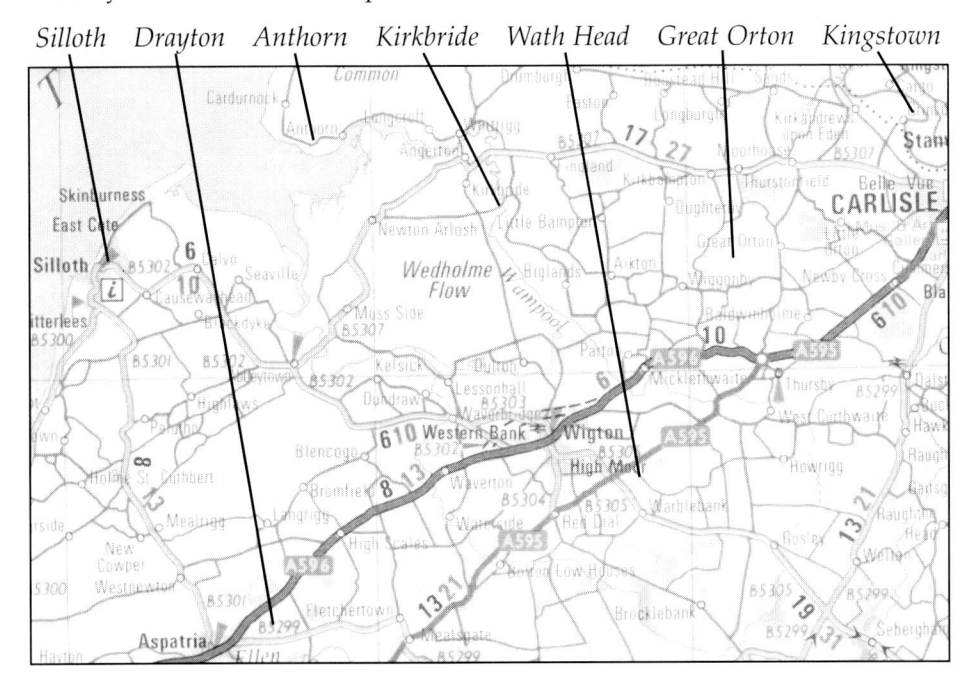

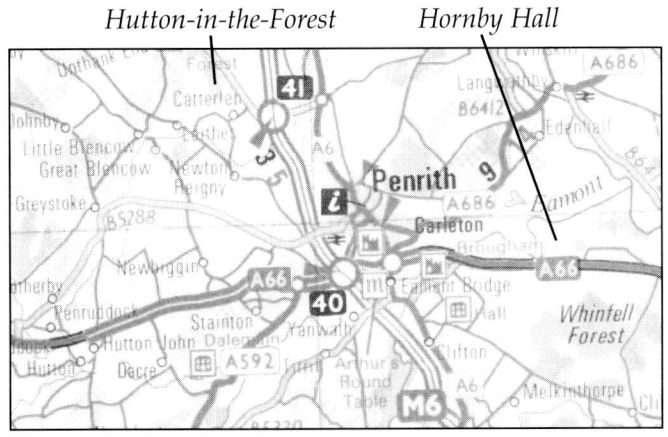

SILLOTH

Opened: September 1939.
Closed: 1960.
O.S. Map Ref.: NY125540.
Runways: Three when active.

Opened as a Coastal Command airfield plus 22 MU. An extremely active wartime airfield which continued to have occasional civil movements after official closure in 1960.

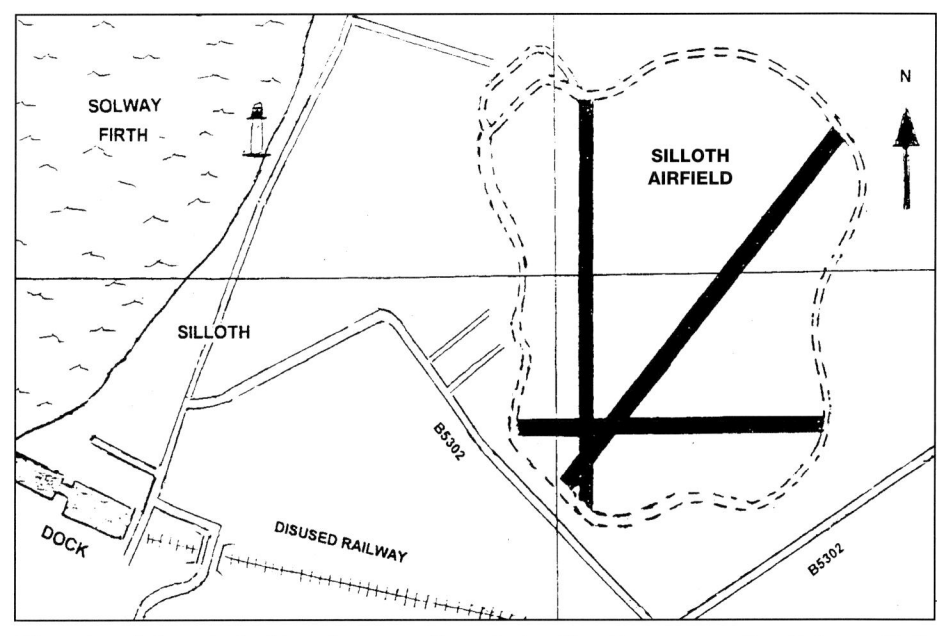

The view below is looking in a north-easterly direction across the Solway Firth towards Scotland. A few hangars remain on the site, most of which is now taken up by industry.

WHY SILLOTH?

The airfield at Silloth was built as a maintenance base and opened in June 1939, twelve weeks before the declaration of the Second World War. Its geographical position a few hundred yards from the Solway's southern shore with a clear aspect over the Irish Sea made it an ideal site for Coastal Command and for an alliance between the two commands during the early part of its active live.

Other units also stayed there for varying periods, among them one from the RAE at Farnborough to try out some very powerful flares carried by a flight of Hampden bombers which were supposed to light up enemy bombers. The problem was that the very purpose they were designed for had precisely the opposite effect: the lights attracted an enemy raider which immediately bombed Silloth. This made the unit somewhat less than popular as the airfield was built where it was to be as far as possible from enemy activity. No tears were shed when it was taken away.

Mk I Handley Page Hampden similar to those from the RAE which were so unpopular at Silloth with their floodlight tests.

Among the first bombers to pass through Silloth for allocation to operational units were Vickers Wellingtons.

The Wellingtons shared the field with the Coastal Command Hudsons and many other types, ranging from Spitfires, Hurricanes, Venturas, Beauforts, Yorks, Liberators, Fortresses and Lancasters. At the end of hostilities, as the military use ran down, short-lived civil passenger services were tried out until the present Carlisle airport was opened. Even after that, some private operators continued to use the site for a year or so when it closed in the 1960s.

AIRCRAFT TYPES FLOWN FROM SILLOTH

Lockheed Hudsons were so common when the station got under way that it was the type that most think of when they think of Silloth. A great deal of test and other flights were made over the adjacent Solway Firth and there were so many ditchings that the Firth became known as 'Hudson Bay' to hundreds of servicemen stationed there. The fact of the matter was that between No. 22 MU, at least two OTUs and Coastal Command, the airfield was hopelessly over-crowded and many of the aircraft based and stored there had to park and operate from the satellite strips, of which at least four were built within twenty miles of Silloth.

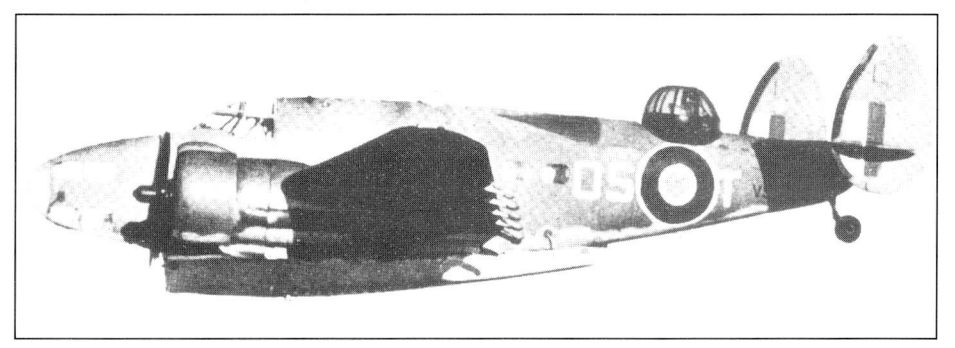

Lockheed Hudsons of Coastal Command were maintained and flown from Silloth.

The ubiquitous Auster seemed to turn up just about anywhere there was a landing ground. Certainly in the Second World War they were in and out of Silloth almost every day it was possible to fly. After the war a number of privately and club-owned civil ones were operated from Silloth, and the author enjoyed an interesting two-hour flight over Lakeland in the 1960s, a short time before the field closed to aviation.

The Taylorcraft Auster was mainly used for communications and army co-operation.

THE WAR-TIME YEARS OF KIRKBRIDE

Opened: May 1939.
Closed: For Military use 1960.
O.S. Map Ref.: NY225550. Nine miles W of Carlisle.
Runways: Three in 1939, only main E/W 10/28, 4,000 ft still in use.

The full story of Kirkbride would fill a book on its own. It was built mainly for storage and as a maintenance unit to keep aircraft being delivered from factories until they could be accepted by the units to which they would be allocated. The concept of this was forced upon the nation when everybody realised in 1938 that impending war was unavoidable. It made sense to the powers that be that the increasing flow of aircraft from the factories should be kept as far as practical from where the action would occur until they were ready for service, and Cumberland as it was then hosted four main bases and a further four satellites, of which Kirkbride was one of the busiest.

In the first two years of Kirkbride's active life it became so busy that the civilian ATA (Air Transport Auxiliary) formed a Ferry Pilots' Pool (No. 16 FPP) on the site to cope with the increasing comings and goings. Their local base was set up in what is now the White Heather Hotel, which is very much involved with the local flying club that keeps the field active for private flyers sixty years later.

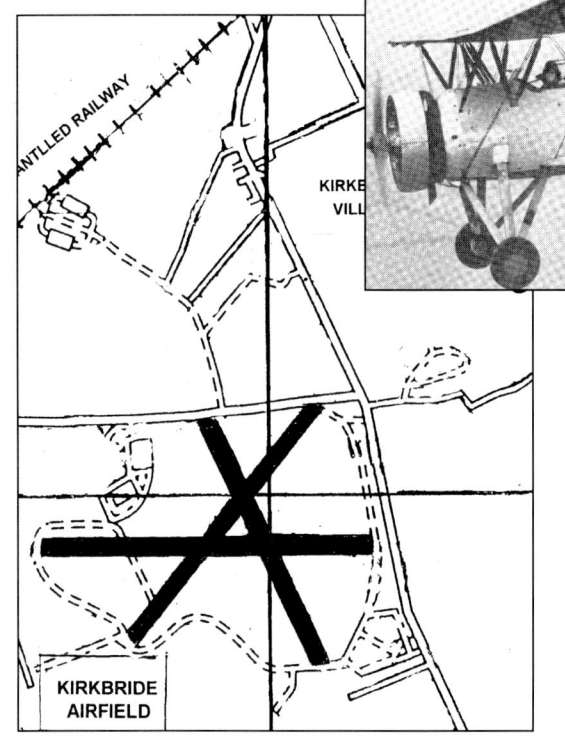

Four Avro Tutors, similar to the one above, were delivered by rail to Kirkbride. Why these aircraft in particular were chosen and to what purpose they were intended is not recorded.

War-time air activity was increased by the formation of No. 12 MU (Maintenance Unit) which must have dealt with just about every type of service aircraft that flew between 1939 and 1960.

To list all the different types handled by No. 12 MU would be rather pointless in a book of this nature, but it is sufficient to say that they varied from the smallest (such as single-engined Austers and Magisters) to the largest and heaviest, like the four-engined Liberators and Handley Page Halifaxes.

Shortly after the Tutors arrived, two Magisters were delivered – how is not recorded! However, the full flow started shortly afterwards with Fairey Battles straight from the factory in primer paint, so it is assumed that a paint job was one of the first that came the way of the airfield staff or the newly formed MU.

The problem with the Fairey Battle was that it had become out-dated by the time the Second World War had broken out. It was basically a good aircraft which had been overtaken by developments.

It was the existence of the Maintenance Unit that turned this sleepy corner of the Cumberland countryside into one of the busiest areas of aviation in the country. For seven or eight years Kirkbride was well and truly on the aviation map!

TYPICAL EVERY-DAY CONTRAST THAT WOULD HAVE BEEN SEEN AT 12 MU AT KIRKBRIDE

Handley Page Halifax heavy bombers were no strangers to this Cumbrian airfield. This particular example was from a Free-French squadron and fitted with H2S radar in the ventral blister. This radar gave a map-type display of the area over which the aircraft was passing.

Of all the fighter aircraft in the RAF the Spitfire was the one that all pilots loved. The ATA ferry pilots based at Kirkbride could easily have been detailed to fly the Halifax out to its operational station and bring back the Spitfire for service or modification. Such was a typical contrast that would have been all in a day's work for them.

Such was the variation of types passing through Kirkbride that the problem which arose was how to find the pilots to collect or deliver them. This was brought about by the mushrooming of production and there not being enough spare pilots because they were needed for active service. The shortage suddenly became very urgent at the outbreak of the Second World War and it led to the formation of pools of civilian pilots being established across the UK. It was No. 16 Ferry Pilots' Pool (16 FPP) that was based at Kirkbride.

FERRY PILOTS AT KIRKBRIDE

No. 12 MU was the unit that was the reason for hundreds of aircraft being brought to Kirkbride and its satellite airfields nearby, and then sending them off to various other units when they were ready. The vast majority of these aircraft were flown in or out by one of the six hundred pilots of the ATA, of which one hundred and fifty were female.

Pilots and staff of the No. 16 Ferry Pilots' Pool in front of an Avro Anson they used as a taxi aircraft to get them from one assignment to another, outside their local base which is now the White Heather Hotel. One wonders if the Sunday lunches they are proud of today were as good in those bad old days of rationing!

This ATA pilot is seen signing to take over a Hudson Bomber before delivering it to its assigned unit, which could have been ten miles down the coast at Silloth or somewhere in Cornwall. Whichever, to an ATA pilot it was all in a day's work, for the next job could well have been to ferry a Flying Fortress or Spitfire from Cornwall and take it to Lincoln on the way back.

COMMUNICATION AIRCRAFT AT KIRKBRIDE

With so many comings and goings it was not unusual for ATA pilots, having made a delivery, to find themselves away from base without transport back. For this reason there was a small fleet of taxi planes, ferries for ferry pilots, typical examples of which are shown on this page.

The Percival Proctor communications aircraft as used by the RAF and ATA.

The Argus, an American light aircraft as used on communication duties by the USAF, RAF and ATA.

Often seen at Kirkbride, the Avro Anson 'Faithful Annie' of which well over 8,000 were built and used in various forms by the ATA, RAF and many other Air Forces.

POST-WAR YEARS AT KIRKBRIDE

At the end of the Second World War in Europe, thousands of aircraft were redundant and the ATAs were disbanded without any real recognition for the work they had done. Service pilots were found to do all the ferry work carried out in the war years by the ATA, and airfields like Kirkbride became gigantic parking places for unwanted aircraft. No. 12 MU itself had some work left and the field was kept going in a reduced way for a further ten or twelve years, when it was virtually abandoned by the Services and left to rot until bought by a private owner who kept it alive by maintaining the main runway and turning the old ATA base into the White Heather Hotel.

We have to say that to list the aircraft types that were seen at Kirkbride is not possible within the confines of these pages. Pictures of the field's wartime activities are hard to come by, but a few about the ATA which performed a demanding and vital job at Kirkbride and elsewhere have been included. The picture above gives an indication of the magnitude of the work left when hostilities ceased. The remarkable view of Kirkbride was taken about 1947 from 8,000 feet when the field's main use was for storage of unwanted aircraft awaiting disposal. The caption of the original picture, which is from an old newspaper clipping, says that at the time it was taken there were over 1,200 aircraft stored there.

SOME OF THE AIRCRAFT DEALT WITH BY THE MUs

Handley Page Halifax Mk I, many of which were prepared for action at Kirkbride.

Grumman Hellcat, still in American markings, before delivery to Anthorn to be anglicised and equipped to meet full Royal Navy needs.

The Hawker Hurricane was the mainstay of the RAF's eight-gun fighters at the outbreak of WW2. There were not many of the Cumbrian MUs or airfields that did not play host to considerable numbers of these great fighter aircraft at some time in their active lives.

SATELLITE AND DISPERSAL AIRFIELDS

Just before and shortly after the outbreak of World War II the programme of airfield building was going apace. In Cumberland the first two at Silloth and Kirkbride were envisaged as storage and maintenance units, away from the anticipated action in the south-east of the country. A little later five others were planned and in the event only four built. These were Crosby on Eden, Longtown, Great Orton and Anthorn, which all served the purpose for which they were planned. The odd one out was Anthorn as it was used entirely for the Navy and not the RAF, mainly for operational training units.

Three large Maintenance Units (MUs) were set up: No. 22 at Silloth and No. 12 at Kirkbride; No. 14 was at Carlisle adjacent to Kingstown airfield, although officially it was a separate base. These soon brought in so much work that the airfields themselves could not cope. This led to a detailed search for suitably flat sites (a rarity in Cumberland) for dispersal fields where aircraft could be stored and if necessary have basic work carried out.

These were never envisaged as anything better than overflow aircraft parks although, in spite of being little better than large fields, in the few years they were active they served a vital purpose. There is very little left today to mark these sites as short-lived but busy airfields. There are one or two old hangars left, now used as barns or storage for farm machinery, and even buildings that once served as temporary watch offices (at the time 'watch towers' would have been too grand a name for them).

This view of the landing strip at Hutton-in-the-Forest is typical of what can be seen today at many of the temporary dispersal air strips set up in the war years. The difference at Hutton was that the line of the strip was nearly due north, which made it cross-wind for all approaches from the air.

During the war years photography was forbidden, and the simplicity of the sites meant that the return to nature or their original use was rapid and is now all but complete. For this reason the theme of 'before and after' cannot be illustrated in this book, as all that could be shown would be a field as it is today! However, just to prove the point, the picture above shows the landing strip at Hutton-in-the-Forest as it is today, which is fairly typical of all of the old satellite sites.

BRAYTON / BRAYTON PARK

Opened: May 1942.
Closed: December 1945.
Grass Airfield: Opened as SLG 39.
O.S. Map Ref.: NY172425.
Runways: Nil permanent.

Satellite Landing Ground (SLG) 39 for 12 MU at Kirkbride was also known as Brayton Park and sited approximately one mile east of Aspatria near Maryport and is probably one of the more interesting airfields of this type in Cumberland. The points that made it a cut above the others were that, right from the start, local opposition to it being built at all delayed its completion for over a year, in spite of the wartime emergency.

This, added to an urgent requirement to carry out work on Halifax bombers, which meant the Wellingtons at Kirkbride had to be moved to Brayton, had a truly remarkable effect on Brayton. At one time over two hundred aircraft were crowded onto the site, fences had to be erected to keep cattle away from the aircraft, dummy fences were painted onto the landing strips and new places had to be sited to hide many of the aircraft sent there. It will be noticed that landing 'strips', plural, are referred to because Brayton had two, which in itself was unusual for a small dispersal field, and if this wasn't enough one of these had to be lengthened to give an over-run for aircraft with dodgy brakes and to cope with some of the later and heavier types that were beginning to use the field.

Because Brayton was the first dispersal field in Lakeland to accept aircraft with a tricycle undercarriage, and any pictures from these fields are very hard to come by, we take the liberty of including this one which is a genuine Mitchell bomber on another airfield.

Boeing Flying Fortresses were by this time being handled for Coastal Command at Kirkbride, as were Spitfires and Vultee Vengeances, and it wasn't long before these could all be seen at Brayton together with a multitude of Wellingtons. One of the more interesting aircraft for the enthusiast must have been the North American B25 Mitchell bombers, as they were among the first aircraft with a tricycle nose wheel undercarriage to use the field. Elsewhere in this book (*p. 39*) is an aerial view of Kirkbride taken about 1947, showing what must have been most of the aircraft that were moved there when Brayton closed, in December 1945. Today there are a few relics, including an old Robin hangar, but little else to indicate the site's four hectic years.

WATH HEAD

Opened: February 1941.
Closed: September 1945.
Designated: SLG 10.
O.S. Map Ref.: NY295480. Approx. one mile E of Wigton and seven miles SW of Carlisle.
Runways: None known but may have had pierced steel planking emplaced temporarily to cope with a winter flooding situation.

Opened as dispersal airfield for 12 MU at Kirkbride in much the same way as Brayton, and after trial landings, various aircraft including three or four dozen Handley Page Hampdens were flown in for storage. In the first winter flooding became so bad that the field had to be closed while the problem was resolved. Apart from the flooding two events of note are recorded about Wath Head. The first was the great British public moaned because the white fuselage of the Coastal Command aircraft being handled by Kirkbride and stored at Wath Head made the airfield (which was supposed to be secret) stand out like a sore thumb. The 'powers that be' agreed and it was arranged that these aircraft would be covered with camouflage netting when out in the open. A problem also arose with a sabotage scare which in fact resolved itself, as aircraft were moved to Hornby Hall and Brayton while the flooding problem was sorted out. Virtually nothing is left today to show the scenes of activity more than half a century ago.

All the fuss the authorities and local people made at Wath Head about Flying Fortresses standing out like a sore thumb in the verdant Cumbrian countryside on what was supposed to be a secret airfield can be understood by looking at the one above. It isn't white as the Coastal Command colour scheme was; the one above is silver, but it still stands out! Oh yes, the author cheats, just a little – the one in the picture is a Flying Fortress, but 300 miles south of Cumbria at Blackbushe some fifty years after Wath Head closed. It has been included because it illustrates the text.

HUTTON-IN-THE-FOREST

Opened: June 1941.
Closed: August 1945.
Airfield: Satellite Landing Ground, mainly for Silloth.
O.S. Map Ref.: NY470350. S of B5305 Wigton road, three miles NW of Penrith.
Runways: Grass strips.

Built as a satellite airfield for Silloth, designated SLG 8, to be used mainly for storage and dispersal of aircraft for 22 MU (Maintenance Unit). In the first instance the main types consisted of Blackburn Bothas, Bristol Blenheims, Hawker Hurricanes and later Lockheed Venturas and P51 Mustang fighters. It was never an easy site for landings and take-offs as the line of the longest grass runway was predominately cross-wind, but later larger aircraft such as Wellington and Stirling bombers were seen on the field. As the author passed the site nearly every day in its last few months of active life, it is known that most of these left by road in pieces. Little remains to be seen today except for what is left of the butts used for testing guns.

The remains of the gun synchronising butts in the north-west corner of the dispersal landing ground at Hutton-in-the-Forest where eight-gun fighters could be tested to ensure all guns concentrated their fire at the point where they would do most damage.

Airspeed's faithful twin-engined trainer, the Oxford, was frequently seen flying in and out of Hutton-in-the-Forest almost up to the day the field closed.

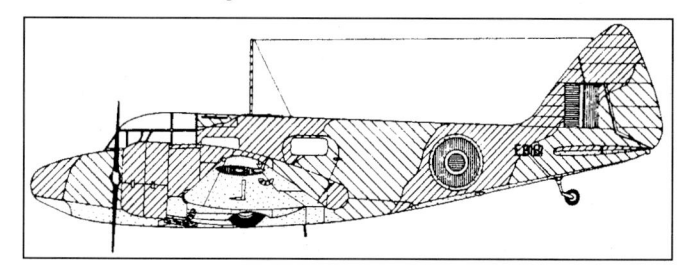

HORNBY HALL

Opened: March 1941.
Closed: July 1945.
Airfield: Satellite landing and dispersal ground for Silloth and designated as SLG 9 under control of 22 MU.
O.S. Map Ref.: NY575295. N of A66, four miles E of Penrith.
Runways: Nil. Grass strips and some areas of pierced steel planking.

Hornby Hall was one of the best kept secrets of Lakeland. There are many stories about it being so well hidden that some aircraft missed it entirely, as the natural cover of the trees hid the aircraft stored there. This natural camouflage was so effective that from the air and the ground most who passed close by every day didn't realise there was an airfield there. The author used to swim in the river Eamont, a mile or so upstream from Hornby Hall, and while he recalls seeing many Hurricanes and Hudsons flying around what he now knows was Hornby Hall, it wasn't until many years later he heard it was an airfield. In fact many thought it was a Prisoner of War camp – which indeed it was, but only after it was officially closed as an airfield.

Another local connection which only came the author's way in the last few weeks before this book went to print was that the father of a good friend, both of whom were known to him, used to be in the Home Guard and frequently had duties at Hornby Hall.

Today there is little left (apart from an old Robin hangar used as a barn and a few other minor buildings) to show that for three years dozens of Lockheed Hudsons, Fairey Battles, Blackburn Bothas, Bristol Blenheims, Vickers Wellingtons and Hawker Hurricanes were on the field at any one time – presumably just for storage, as most were obsolete by 1943.

AIRCRAFT TYPES TO BE SEEN AT ANY OF THE ABOVE AIRFIELDS AT SOME PERIOD DURING WORLD WAR II

Airspeed Oxford	Handley Page Halifax	NA P51 Mustang
Avro Anson	Handley Page Hampden	NA B25 Mitchell
Blackburn Botha	Hawker Hurricane	Short Stirling
Boeing B17 Fortress	Lockheed Hudson	Supermarine Spitfire
Bristol Blenheim	Lockheed Ventura	Vickers Wellington
DH Tiger Moth	Miles Magister	Vultee Vengeance
Fairey Battle		

It must be emphasised that the above list is of aircraft that the author can confirm from personal sightings or from those persons he has spoken to, such as a number of ATA pilots who remember having visited them at some time between 1941 and 1945. It does not apply to other than the dispersal fields and is only quoted to indicate that the temporary sites handled many an aircraft one wouldn't normally have expected to see in such unlikely spots.

GREAT ORTON

Opened: June 1943.
Closed: 1952.
O.S. Map Ref.: NY310540. Seven miles WSW of Carlisle.
Runways: Three (one rather longer than usual for the time).

There seems to have been some confusion over what Great Orton was for. It was first envisaged as a satellite for Silloth with the idea of transfer to Crosby. It would seem that this was one of those 'good ideas at the time' that came to nothing because another airfield, planned to be under Silloth's control at Mawbray a few miles down the coast, six miles north of Maryport, was never built. In the event Silloth then decided to make use of the field for the Wellingtons of an OTU which needed more space than Silloth could spare.

Although Great Orton was built for a different reason, it ended up being what was virtually a satellite of Silloth, put to use by No. 6 OTU's Vickers Wellington bombers, similar to the one in the illustration above.

Great Orton itself was not fully completed until the end of 1943, some six months after its official opening when some Hurricanes arrived from the OTU at Longtown in the October of 1943, followed by a conversion squadron for Typhoon fighter bombers, formed in the April of the following year.

Typhoon fighter bombers getting sorted out on arrival at the airfield in the Spring of 1944 to join a new conversion squadron formed to develop aggressive tactics, for which Typhoons were found to be very suitable, being called for by fighter bombers.

GREAT ORTON'S UNUSUALLY LONG RUNWAY

The map shows the conventional layout of the runways at Great Orton but the NE/SW one was unusually long and probably indicated that the site was planned for greater things.

By the time Great Orton was complete, the RAF was facing the situation of how to switch from the defensive. The Battle of Britain was over, and the return to Europe on the offensive was absolute priority in everybody's thinking. The application of existing aircraft and a number of new ones to the new strategy led to some unusual units, with a variety of old and new aircraft arriving and departing more often than one would expect for a site of this nature.

The plan of Great Orton airfield shows it being of what had become the conventional layout for the times. But it was different in that the main runway was longer than normal, which would normally indicate that users would in the main be heavier aircraft which required a greater take-off or landing run.

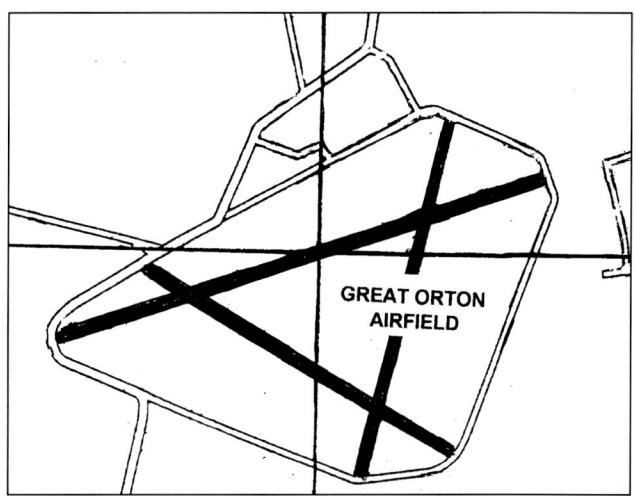

Vickers Warwick Air Sea Rescue aircraft with parachutable lifeboat in a ventral pod.

The Vickers Warwick was designed to replace the Wellington bomber but was obsolete before it could be put into service, so a number were converted to Search and Rescue aircraft and carried a lifeboat which could be dropped to anyone found stranded at sea. A number of these aircraft served on detachment to Great Orton for missions over the Irish Sea.

A DIFFERENT TASK

In the two or three years when Great Orton could be considered as an 'action station' it must have been an interesting airfield, for it played host to a wide variety of units and aircraft. Even in its dying days it was given a very different task by a Maintenance Unit that had the job of storing unwanted bombs until 1952. Locals who knew this didn't exactly give it their approval.

Yet another use for Great Orton has been discovered four and a half decades after its final abandonment by officialdom: that of power generation. There have been attempts to revive some commercial activity even to the extent that aviation activities here refuse to die. Parts of the old taxiways have been used for microlight training from time to time.

Even when active, some airfields look miserable on a bad day and Great Orton is no exception. The remains of the old watch tower doesn't make it look better either. The line of wind generators gives it a 'windmill land' look that at least shows the old airfield still has some usefulness left in it.

It is noted at the beginning of this story of Great Orton that it became what it was when another nearby airfield project was cancelled. In a convoluted way it is what it is because another airfield project was never taken up, only in this case that cancellation resulted more directly in the rather dismal scene we have today. This was the rejection of the plan to turn Great Orton into Carlisle's City Airport in favour of Crosby on Eden.

By coincidence, and literally as these words were being written, the author had a phone call from a Cumbrian friend who informed him that Carlisle's airport had just been sold to a private businessman on the understanding that it should be kept open for ten years. One wonders if the same would have happened if Great Orton had become the City's airport and not Crosby.

In fact, almost a 'Stop Press' situation has since occurred, and one which no-one would have wished for. In April 2001, just before this chapter went to the printers, Northern Cumbria (the main area covered by this book) was afflicted by a massive outbreak of Foot and Mouth Disease – and a sad use for Great Orton became the burning and disposal of slaughtered animals. Not at all what one would have hoped for as a use of this part of our aviation heritage.

ANTHORN (ex *HMS NUTHATCH*)

Opened: September 1944 as RN airfield *HMS Nuthatch*.
Closed: c. 1960 to aviation.
O.S. Map Ref.: NY180580. WNW of Carlisle.
Runways: Three when built.

In several ways Anthorn was different from all the other Cumbrian airfields. It was the last to be built and the only pure Naval air station with the prime job of preparing aircraft for naval use. With shades of the naval traditions and shades of memories of the *Mayfly* saga of 1909 (*see page 5*), it was given a ship's title, *HMS Nuthatch*, and the staff (sorry, crew) went ashore and not into town! Inevitably it was known as a 'Stone Frigate'.

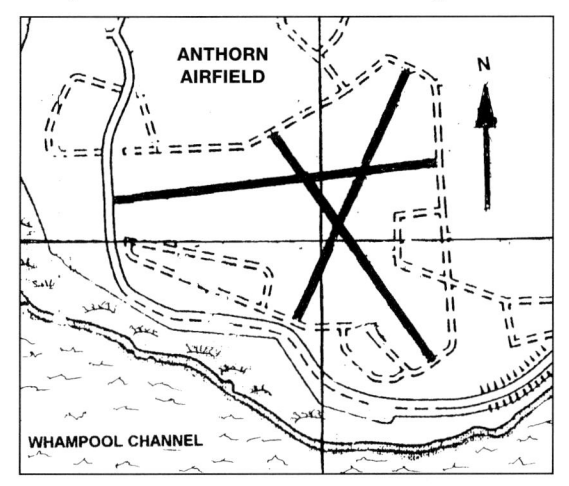

A point came when the Navy had to give way to the accumulated knowledge of aviators in the format of an airfield on dry land which, unlike an aircraft carrier, could not be turned into wind and therefore had to have three runways. No longer needed for aviation, the Navy has found another use for Anthorn, as a radio communication station.

SOME OF THE AIRCRAFT TYPES HANDLED AT ANTHORN

Anthorn was in its own way the Naval equivalent of the RAF's Maintenance Units and the different types of aircraft it handled are so many that it is only possible to mention a few. At the start most were delivered by pilots of the ATA, but later, when hostilities of the Second World War ceased, service pilots and those from the manufacturers were used.

It is difficult to consider two more contrasting aircraft types than those depicted on this page, but the Navy, being what it was, had a go at anything once it was convinced that it would serve a purpose.

The Navy's venerable Fairey Swordfish. Obsolete when World War II broke out, it gave successful active service to the very end of hostilities. The aircraft in the illustration above is still flying in the Royal Navy's Historic Aircraft Flight.

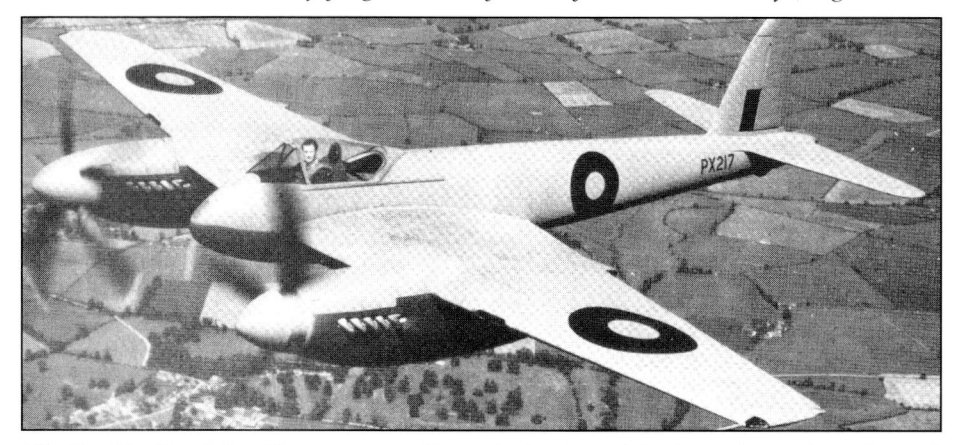

The De Haviland Sea Hornet was a direct derivation of the legendary Mosquito and a number of them passed through Anthorn to be prepared for service with the Navy.

OTHER NAVAL AIRCRAFT THAT WERE TO BE SEEN AT ANTHORN IN ITS ACTIVE LIFE AS AN AIRFIELD

The Swordfish's replacement, the Barracuda, was indeed a complicated aircraft compared with those it was replacing, but after some major initial problems brought about by being under-powered, more powerful engines turned it into a moderately successful aircraft until replaced by even more modern designs in the late 1940s and early 1950s.

The Fairey Barracuda was designed to be a naval dive and torpedo bomber as a replacement for the old Swordfish and Albacore aircraft.

A Hawker Sea Fury, one of many that passed through Anthorn's care.

Both the Swordfish and the Sea Fury are still flying today in the the Royal Navy's Historic Flight and can be seen on show at numerous air displays around the country many times in most years. In their day they were to be seen in the Lakeland skies on their way to or from Anthorn.

BURNFOOT

Opened: September 1940.
Closed: July 1945.
O.S. Map Ref.: NY375660.
Runways: Nil. All grass airfield.

Within a year of the Second World War breaking out, Kingstown became so overcrowded as an Elementary Training School, mainly flying Miles Magisters and DH Tiger Moths, that a number of detachments were sent to Burnfoot where a crude airfield was set up as relief landing ground. It wasn't very long before this site also became so busy that it came very close to being a unit in its own right.

Another factor that had to be taken into account as time went by was the closeness of Longtown and Crosby on Eden, with intensive training on heavier and faster aircraft overlapping the skies over Burnfoot. For safety's sake this led to the setting up of zones where individual stations had to restrict their flying activities to allocated areas. The need for the site ended with the war and closure took place in July 1945.

The Miles Magister was one of the most common of the basic training aircraft in use in the 1940s and together with Tiger Moths saw many budding pilots through the first stages of their training at Burnfoot.

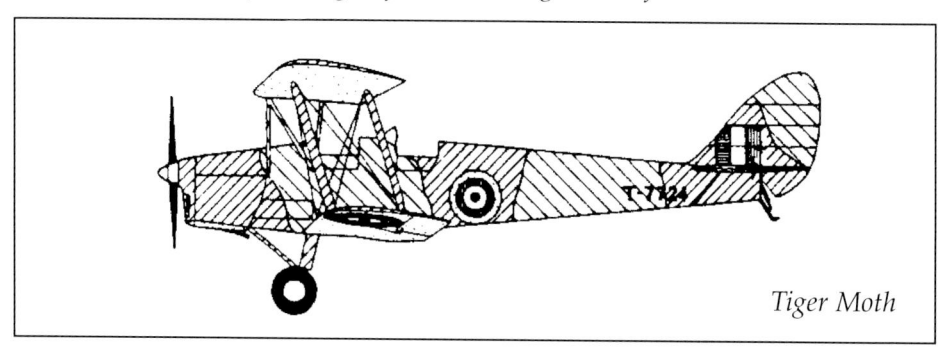

Tiger Moth

LONGTOWN AND CROSBY ON EDEN

Opened: July 1941.
Closed: 1946.
O.S. Map Ref.: NY410683.
Runways: Three, later extension to main runway for training on large aircraft.

Although a large airfield by standards of the times, Longtown was regarded for most of its active life as a satellite for other airfields in the area, in the first instance as a base for the Hurricanes from Crosby on Eden. Most people with long memories seem to remember the Beaufighters and Beauforts operating from there, which certainly caused more than a little congestion in the air over the Solway, especially with the elementary training that was taking place at nearby Burnfoot, Kingstown and Crosby. This led to the setting up of definite areas for the units at each of those airfields.

Longtown airfield from the air about 1942 and looking roughly south-west.

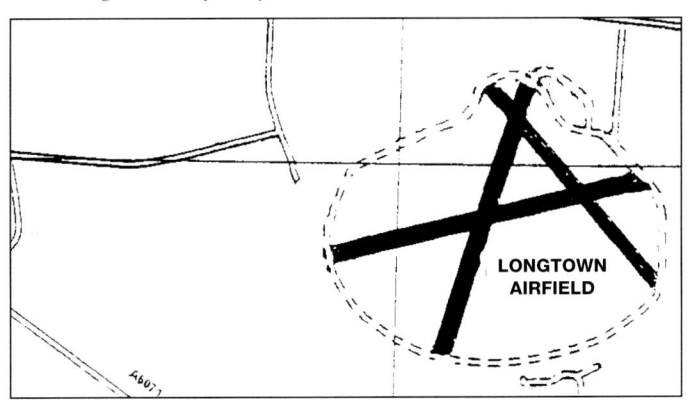

The sketch map makes an interesting comparison with the photograph above.

Drawing of a Bristol Beaufort torpedo bomber, residents of 9 OTU in 1944.

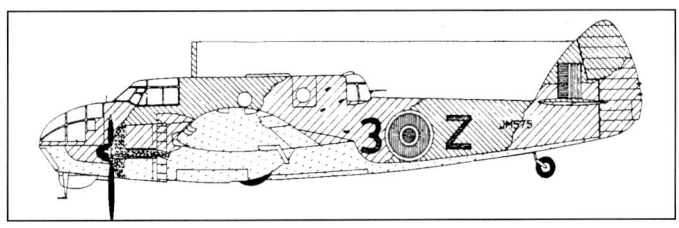

53

The scenes at Longtown were very much like any RAF transport airfield and the work and training carried out there stood the country in good stead a year or so later, when every aircraft that could lift a load into the air was needed on the Berlin Airlift. Phrases like swords into ploughshares come to mind, only in this case it was food and fuel and not bombs.

Liberators, while not common, were often seen at Longtown. The one above was not being prepared for the Berlin Airlift, but probably on a training mission.

The Avro York above may well have been prepared for the airlift and could well have operated from Longtown at the same time as the Liberator. The rain is the same, isn't it?

The two lower pictures are in the same location but fifty years apart. Even the rain has stopped!

THE TWO AVROS

It seems appropriate that both the aircraft types shown on this page should be mentioned in connection with Crosby on Eden and Longtown. They were seen at other Cumbrian airfields over the war years, but were different in this connection because they were actually in units based at these two stations for training purposes and not just for maintenance or storage.

Longtown and Crosby on Eden were built early in the Second World War as training airfields. Longtown had a runway that was quite long in those days, so lent itself well later for converting aircrew to heavy aircraft. In its five years of operational life it was host to such aircraft as Spitfires, Hurricanes, Beaufighters, Stirlings, Fortresses, Liberators, Dakotas and others.

The Avro Lancaster, pictured above, was one of the RAF's most successful bombers and many of its constituent parts such as the wings, engines and tail units were used in Avro's transport version, the York, shown below. The ventral blister underneath contained the H2S radar that gave map-like displays which became a great aid to identifying its targets.

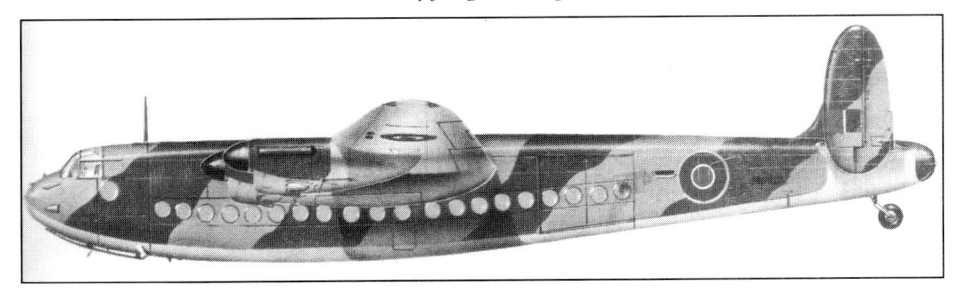

Crosby followed a similar pattern to Longtown, but concentrated more on training of long-range fighter crews and only towards the end of its active life as an RAF station did it compliment Longtown in the training of crews for heavier aircraft, when many of that type of aircraft were using both stations.

Unlike Longtown, which seemed to have been left to rot, Crosby had a new lease of life given when in the 1960s it became Carlisle's airport and has been developed and maintained into what it is today.

CROSBY ON EDEN

Opened: February 1941.
Closed: By RAF, May 1946.
O.S. Map Ref.: NY480610.
Runways: Three (when built).

Aerial view taken c.1942 from approx. 8,000 feet on a westerly approach and before the east/west runway was extended.

This sketch map shows the familiar layout of wartime airstations. When Crosby first opened it was a bit of a mess and facilities were minimal, as can be seen from the aerial view above. However, within a few weeks trainee pilots were starting to learn on various fighter aircraft including Beaufighters, like that in the drawing below, which is virtually identical to those at an OTU at Crosby in the early 1940s.

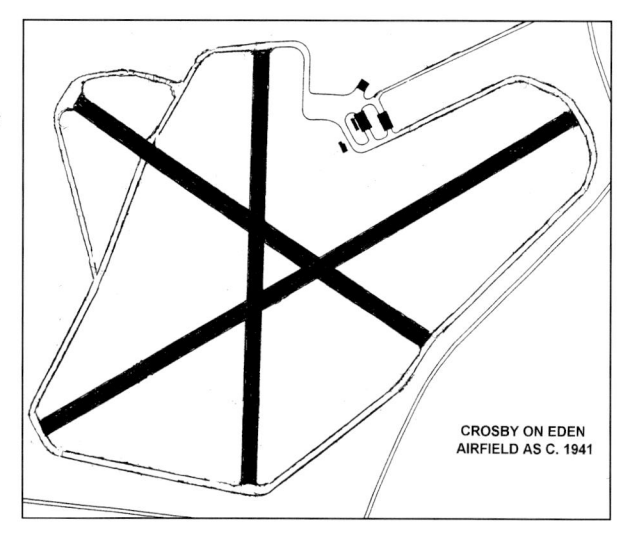

CROSBY ON EDEN
AIRFIELD AS C. 1941

In the four or five years of Crosby's active life as an RAF station it became quite busy, with the advanced training of pilots in the handling of the more sophisticated and heavier aircraft which were being rushed into service as soon as was practical. Because of this there was a great similarity in the types of aircraft of the units that came and went as the war progressed at Crosby and nearby Longtown. In the first couple of years much of the training for day fighter pilots was carried out on ex Battle of Britain Hurricanes, including Free-French pilots. The picture below shows one occasion in 1941 when General de Gaulle carried out an inspection of the station.

The second phase of the station's life was dictated by Beaufighter, Beaufort and an air firing conversion unit to be based there, and the runways were extended to cater for heavier and faster aircraft. The advantages of this became obvious later when sixteen Lancaster bombers were diverted to Crosby after a raid on the Rhur, when they could not return to their own base. Later still, towards the end of the war, the need for transport aircraft brought units of Dakotas, Stirlings and Yorks to Crosby.

A conversion of a Short Stirling bomber into a transport aircraft. This was used to bring refugee Czech children away from war-torn Europe to a more peaceful Cumberland, as it was then known.

CARLISLE (Ex CROSBY ON EDEN)

RAF Station: Crosby on Eden (February 1941 to May 1946).
Closed: July 1945.
Re-opened: Officially in June 1960 as Carlisle City Airport.
O.S. Map Ref.: NY480610. Approx. five miles ENE of Carlisle.
Runways: Three when built (NE-SW 07/25 and N-S 19/01 still in use).

An ex RAF airfield, now Carlisle's City Airport. One of the smaller regional airports with no scheduled services at the time of writing, it is well equipped to deal with seasonal charters and corporate aircraft, with a terminal building that satisfies most needs. Based there are some very active flying schools which offer a wide range of training facilities, and an interesting museum and aviation heritage centre that attracts many visitors.

When the RAF built Crosby as a fighter station it had three runways which were extended two or three years later.

The northern boundary coincided with the line of Hadrian's Wall, built two thousand years before the airfield, which is unfortunately not obvious from the map.

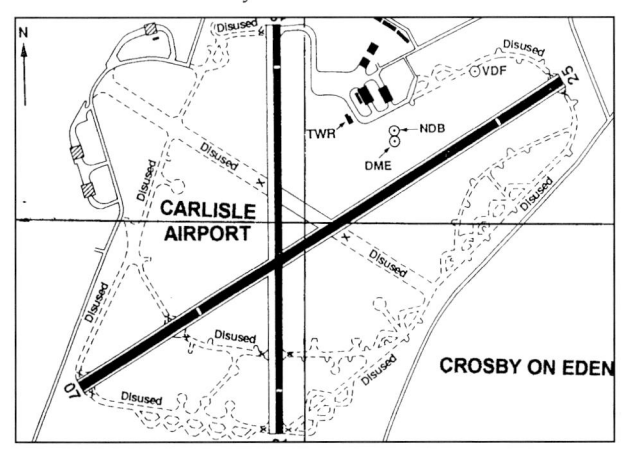

Even after the RAF abandoned the airfield and before Carlisle's City Council bought it to replace Kingstown, BEA used the field for a few flights to the Isle of Man with DH Rapide aircraft like the one above.

THE PLANE THAT WILL NOT DIE

Sixty plus years ago the author was waiting to board a Handley Page biplane airliner at Croydon to fly to Paris with his father when a gleaming Swissair DC3 landed and parked alongside the HP42 we were to fly in. My father, who had been a flyer all his working life, remarked when he saw the DC3 to the effect that "There is a plane ten years ahead of its time". I believed him, although neither he nor I knew his sums were six decades out.

Ten years after the first DC3 left the Douglas factory, many thousand aircraft of this type were flying in both civil and military format. The C47s seen in the above picture carried the famous invasion stripes which were all part of the preparation for 'D' Day in 1944. Many, both British and American Air Force aircraft of this type, were prepared in this way at the Lakeland airfields, including Crosby.

Yet another ten years on, in the early nineteen fifties, the faithful DC3, C47, now known the world over as Dakotas, were still flying from Crosby/Carlisle City and hundreds of other airports for dozens of airlines. Today in the third millennium a few are still flying! It is now hoped they will never die.

CARLISLE CITY AIRPORT

Although not orientated in the same direction as the map on page 58, the runway configuration and other details of the airfield are obvious from this aerial view. A look at the aerial picture of the airfield in its first year of operation in 1942 on a previous page shows the considerable clean-up of the site as a city airport.

The control tower and terminal buildings at Carlisle are well equipped and adequate for the traffic levels of the present day, including Customs facilities.

1960s & '70s AT CARLISLE CITY AIRPORT

The 1960s and '70s were years of great hope. The development of specialised passenger aircraft was benefiting from the development of turbo-prop aero engines. This was also helped by a pool of ex Service pilots who only had to re-learn their flying skills to the extent that they had to absorb the growing rules and regulations that governed civil aviation. Carlisle had its fair share of these aircraft through being used in a number of scheduled internal and seasonal schedules which were set up in those two decades.

The fact that Carlisle also benefited from uncluttered airspace well away from the more southerly counties, and being well equipped with the necessary facilities, made it ideal for flying training. The result of this was that a number of flying schools set themselves up on the airport, using training aircraft of the type such as those pictured below.

A popular private and training aircraft in the '60s and '70s, the Beagle Pup, used by the flying school at Carlisle. The RAF trainer version of the Pup was the Beagle Bulldog, also a frequent visitor to Carlisle.

Another Beagle aircraft, the 206, was also based at Carlisle by Casair and many other flying schools elsewhere for twin-engine training.

A legacy of the field's origins is that there is room for expansion, as can be seen in this picture where aircraft of all shapes and sizes had room on the apron in front of the hangars and caused no congestion.

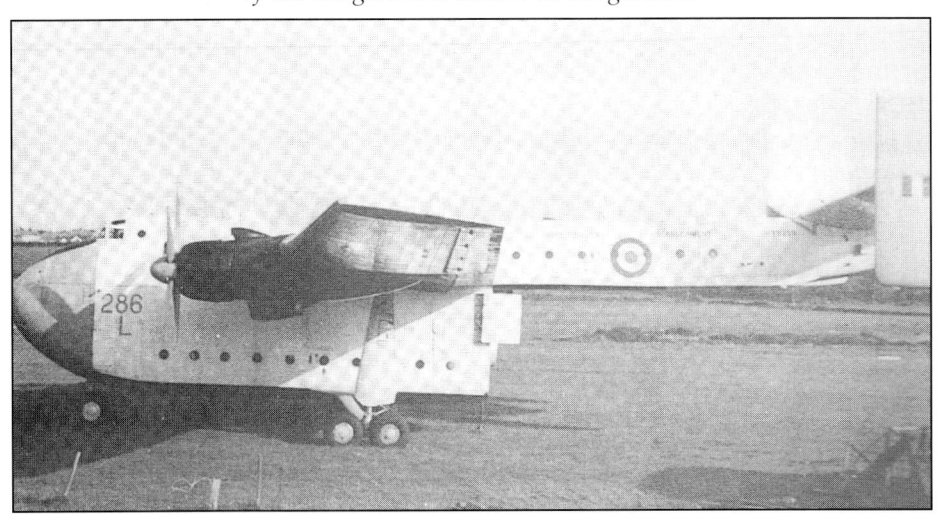

Blackburn Beverley XB286 loading for a cargo flight to Carlisle.

The point made by space being available at Carlisle is well proven because the Blackburn Beverley transport had no problems in delivering its cargo to Carlisle in 1967. The picture above was taken at Sandown, Isle of Wight, when that actual aircraft shown was loaded ready for take off *en route* to Carlisle. The plane was normally based at Farnborough, but had called at Sandown to pick up a Blue Streak rocket, manufactured on the Island at Saunders Roe, to be test-fired at Spadeadam rocket testing ground some miles to the north of Crosby on Eden, which had become Carlisle's airport. The Solway Aviation Society's handbook on Carlisle's airport has a picture of XB261, the above Beverley's sister aircraft, one of the pair that seemed to get this flight whenever needed.

The proliferation of small and medium sized internal airlines with reasonably modern aircraft suited to the envisaged task brought Carlisle a variety of aircraft that delighted the enthusiast but seldom provided a service that was viable.

What Carlisle has lacked in scheduled services it has made up for in a wide variety of one-off visitors. Why this Avro 19 Survey called there in the 1960s is not recorded, but there were a number of national projects, like the natural gas pipeline which benefited to a great extent from the use of aerial surveys. The Avro 19 was probably an ex Service aircraft for which further useful work had been found.

The Avro 748 turbo-prop airliners were popular on medium distance and internal flights. The RAF version was known as the Andover, some of which formed the fixed-wing basis for the planes of the Royal Flight, normally based at RAF Benson in Oxfordshire.

In 1960 when Crosby opened as Carlisle's airport hopes ran high and great efforts were made to attract a good proportion of the growing air traffic market, both seasonal and national. A number of carriers of substantial stature introduced scheduled internal services together with many seasonal charters. Many of these were to the popular resorts in Ireland, the Isle of Man and the Channel Islands. At first the mainstay of these routes was the inevitable Dakota as well as smaller piston-engined aircraft such as the Viking and Heron. Not too long afterwards these were replaced by the more modern, faster and more comfortable prop jets.

Autair was another welcome and for a short while regular visitor to Carlisle. They used the Airspeed Ambassador to make the first call of that type in 1965 and later ones followed when this type was in service as a back-up for other aircraft of that company. Autair, like so many airlines of the time, was short lived mainly due to the fact that lack of viability got the better of them, and they either stopped trading on a large proportion of their routes, were taken over, or just went out of business.

The Vickers Viscount was one of Britain's most successful airliners; over 400 were built and saw service at airports on all five continents, including America – and Carlisle! Its comfort, speed and smoothness made it popular with all who flew in it.

Although the 1970s saw the beginning of the end for scheduled passenger routes to, from and through Carlisle, there were still plenty of other commercial and training activities giving port movements to keep a variety of different aircraft calling and the airport busy.

When the Viscount's younger, but larger, sisters were pensioned off from passenger service, a number of them were converted for cargo work. These were given the name Merchantman and were to be seen at many regional airports, including Carlisle, especially on Saturday evenings when they delivered Sunday papers to the more remote parts and islands around the UK.

This RAF Lockheed Hercules called on a very wet day in 1970. There have been a number of these that still call, usually on some exercise. Carlisle when it was Crosby with the RAF served as a training base for transport aircraft, although it is unlikely that any of the crew of the one above or the present-day were trained there.

From the 1970s onwards the main use of Carlisle's airport was for flying training and corporate aircraft, many in connection with BNFL. In the 1980s Specialist Flying Training operated a fleet of Gazelle helicopters and other aircraft of the advanced trainer type. One of their more lucrative contracts made them less than popular ten years later, when they trained a considerable number of Iraqi pilots not too long before the Kuwait crisis.

In the 1980s the Ministry was assessing the suitability of a number of designs for use as RAF trainers. SFT had the Firecracker, seen above, to assess at Carlisle. In the end the Firecracker was not chosen and the aircraft in the picture was sold to a private owner in America.

One of the highlights of any regional airport must be a royal visit in an aircraft of the Royal Flight, like the Andover above that brought HRH The Prince of Wales to Carlisle to receive the Freedom of the City in January 1986.

Just about seven decades ago Kingstown was proudly opened with the claim that it was the second airfield to be opened as a municipal airport. Since then Carlisle has had variable fortunes when it comes to scheduled routes, but the outbreak of the Second World War brought in another much more lasting activity, that of teaching people to fly. Kingstown was soon bursting at the seams and another airfield at Burnfoot, a few miles to the north, was set up to cope with the wartime-created overflow. This seemed to work very well, but there was a need for still more training facilities and two RAF stations were built and opened at Crosby on Eden and Longtown, both with the main purpose of providing facilities for the training of pilots on aircraft that Kingstown and Burnfoot could not possibly handle.

After the war Burnfoot was redundant and was closed down. Kingstown tried to get back into civil aviation, but soon found that the heavier aircraft which were coming into service in the early 1950s could not be operated from a grass airfield, so it had to be closed down. The inevitable period of discussions and negotiations followed, during which time a few internal services were routed through Crosby on Eden which had by then been abandoned by the RAF. Some tried to use Silloth, and Great Orton was considered as a possibility for the 'New City Airport'. Rightly or wrongly, ten years later the City decided to buy Crosby on Eden and over the next half century has kept it going, giving us what we have today.

The common thread through the whole of the seven decades of flying in northern Cumbria has been flying training. Some took place at Kingstown in the 1930s and it became intense at Kingstown, Burnfoot, Longtown and Crosby in the 1940s, and since 1960 when Carsair used the Beagle aircraft illustrated on a previous page. Since then training has been one of the mainstays of aviation at Crosby as the present City airport.

The Carlisle Flight Centre is the present incumbent at the airport and was formed in 1981 when a group of private pilots joined with Scotia Safari to preserve a private flying organisation at Carlisle. Scotia Safari had much experience with this side of aviation and now have the largest fleet of light aircraft in the north of England and Scotland. It operates most forms of flying training with a fleet of eleven aircraft, including a Grumman Cougar executive twin, Grumman Tigers, Grumman Cheetas, Piper Tomahawks and a Piper Archer.

The title of 'City Airport' was, and still is, a rather grand title for what is a moderately-sized regional airport outside a moderately-sized historic city on the northern edge of Lakeland. However, the linking word is 'historic' for in aviation terms it covers approximately 85% of the history of aviation and even entered that era in 1933 by Kingstown being the second in the country to be licensed as a municipal airport. Less than ten years later Crosby on Eden was built as an RAF airfield and two decades later took on the title as Carlisle's official airport.

The history of Carlisle goes back over two millennium which is in effect equalled by the site of the present airport, for part of its northern boundary is along the line of Hadrian's Wall and there is a site of a Roman camp within the airfield itself.

Large and impressive aircraft are always an attraction and the Vulcan 'V' bomber is certainly an eye-catcher at Carlisle, where it is displayed near the Solway Aviation Museum at the City Airport.

There is now a more recent era of local history for all to see in the form of a collection of preserved aircraft beautifully restored and parked for all to see. These and other aircraft have been gathered together by members of the Solway Aviation Society, a group of enthusiasts who have also assembled a collection of artifacts into a very worthwhile museum that reflects the story of the airfield and aviation in Cumbria.

A view of the Engine Hall in the Solway Aviation Museum at Carlisle City's airport.

The Solway Aviation Museum, while concentrating on memorabilia concerning the airport's past, has a few exhibits which are of great interest. The museum itself has a display depicting unique artefacts which tell of a short-lived attempt by the UK to enter the space race alone. A picture on page 62 shows a Blackburn Beverley transport aircraft which was used to bring the rocket parts from the manufacturer on the Isle of Wight.

Outside there is the collection of preserved aircraft which includes an example of a Gloucester Meteor, the first jet fighter aircraft type to enter service with the RAF.

A display of exhibits of the UK's Blue Streak rocket in the Solway Aviation Museum.

The preserved Meteor at Crosby is an example of the first jet fighter to enter service with the RAF. It seems suitable that in the tradition of many Air Force stations, at Crosby, as an ex RAF base, there should be preserved service aircraft as 'gate guardians', keeping alive memories of the site's service to the nation.

PRESENT-DAY LAKELAND AVIATION

Civil aviation in the Lakeland Counties is now mostly limited to north-south overflights four or five miles above in the strictly controlled airlanes. These do not lend themselves to photography from the ground, nor do they seriously disturb the beauty of what is arguably our favourite National Park. On a clear day they can be seen by their vapour trails and they do nothing to upset the beauty of the district, but are a reminder of the thousands that pass over the Lakes every hour, probably without any knowledge of the attractive countryside they are missing below them.

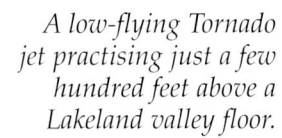

A low-flying Tornado jet practising just a few hundred feet above a Lakeland valley floor.

The picture above is not a cheat but unfortunately the exception to the statements made at the top of the page. It is something that many residents and visitors to Lakeland have seen, heard and many times been startled, if not frightened, by. The military jets practising low flying at two hundred and fifty feet above a valley floor on their way to attack a target can frequently be seen below them by people enjoying the views from a fell top, enabling them to look down on an aircraft in flight.

An entirely different type of flying in Lakeland which visitors and residents alike regard not only as welcome but as an absolute necessity is from RAF and Royal Navy helicopters like the one illustrated above.

PRESENT-DAY LAKELAND AVIATION

Aviation has not entirely deserted Lakeland or Windermere, for Carlisle has turned the old RAF airfield of Crosby on Eden into an airport adequate for the city's needs. A few miles to the west Kirkbride now operates as an airfield for club and private flyers. In South Lakeland, Cark, another ex RAF base, is now operated as the North-West Parachute Centre and to the west of that the industrial interests of Barrow in Furness operate the wartime airfield on Walney Island for their own and visiting corporate aircraft.

In spite of what are entirely legacies of the Second World War to the north and south of the Lake District National Park, central Lakeland has had to succumb to the ubiquitous helicopter and the spread of helipads has made them a feature of many of the more up-market hotels and a number of commercial centres.

Possibly one of the best ways to arrive in the Lakes.

One of the great Victorian industrialists, H. W. Scheneider, might not have agreed with the caption to the picture above because the Belsfield Hotel was once his home and he kept his steam yacht, the *Esperence*, moored just below it. The story goes that every morning his butler took his breakfast to the yacht so that he could enjoy it on the voyage down the lake to Lakeside Station where he would then catch his train to work at Barrow. The *Esperence* can be seen today at the Windermere Steamboat Museum perfectly preserved, together with some other very interesting aviation exhibits.

THE VISIT OF THE LAST SUNDERLAND FLYING BOAT TO WINDERMERE IN 1990

Not all lovers of Lakeland welcomed what they viewed as a 'noisy aeroplane' but the visit of the Sunderland flying boat in 1990 proved unexpectedly popular. This popularity was not just from aviation enthusiasts, for it also brought back memories to quite a number of people who not only remembered those that were built on the lakeside in World War II, but many who had helped build them. Sadly the visiting flying boat was not one of these, but it was still a very welcome visitor.

Some seemed to think this was the Sunderland's last 'fling' at Windermere. In fact it may well have been, which probably contributed to the large number of visitors who enjoyed a boat trip to see a flying boat at close quarters.

It is quite a thought that the Sunderland was about fifty years old when it visited Windermere in 1990 and that the launch acting as tender to the aircraft was probably forty years old when the flying boat visited the lake. It seems that the 'golden oldies' have a lot left in them to give pleasure to all ages.

VISITING SUNDERLAND'S DEPARTURE

The visit of the Sunderland flying boat created a considerable amount of interest from locals as well as visitors. The author was one of a small group responsible for bringing the actual aircraft back to the UK when the owner died in an accident in the Caribbean in one of the other flying boats he owned. The photograph of the flight deck was taken in the actual aircraft just before it was laid up in the Hall of Aviation in Southampton.

The flight deck of the flying boat that visited Windermere in 1990 and what the pilot would see as he prepared for take off.

The view of the visiting flying boat the locals would have seen it as it left Windermere for the last time, its last 'fling' as the local boat company's chalk board implied.

73

KIRKBRIDE TODAY

Kirkbride is now an example of a once busy and important airfield that has survived to provide the present-day requirements of those who are interested enough in aviation to actually take part. The owner of the site went to some trouble and no inconsiderable expense to have the main runway refurbished to a standard that enables its use by a wide range of modern aircraft, albeit with minimal ground-based facilities. Having said that, it lacks one normal activity that makes it very attractive – no landing fee!

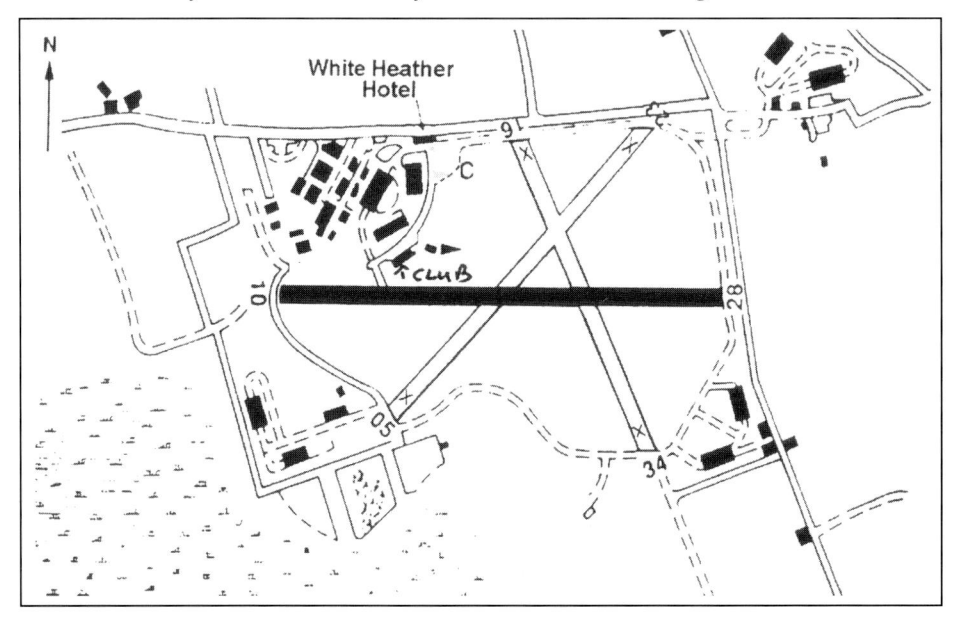

The airfield map above shows the facilities as they are sixty years after the airfield opened. Now in private hands it can still be used, as they say in official jargon, 'at pilots' risk and with the owner's prior permission' as it is not licensed. Recently its use by private aircraft has increased to the extent that it has been allocated its own radio channel on 124.400 MHz with a call sign of 'Kirkbride Radio'.

Another unusual attraction, in addition to that of not charging a landing fee, is marked on the official map as the White Heather Hotel, which was at one time the ATA ferry pilots' Kirkbride base, and is said to serve Sunday lunches which are highly recommended! Nearly all the present activities are co-ordinated by members of the Lorton Aero Club who are mainly responsible for giving the field a new lease of life and a source of enjoyment to members and visitors alike.

The Second World War years were directly and indirectly responsible for the building and operation of well over a thousand airfields in the UK, many of which closed down operationally almost overnight at the end of hostilities. Of those abandoned a few were found other uses, others were left to nature and many of their buildings left to rot. Kirkbride was not given up entirely by the RAF or the MU for some sixteen years after the war was over, which is one reason why so much of its infrastructure can be seen today.

One of the surviving buildings so vital to the airfield when operations were at their peak was the Watch Tower. This is still intact and has been refurbished to serve present-day aviation activities, and in one sense is a museum piece in its own right.

John Plaskett is the co-ordinator of the Lorton Aero Club. He organises the club and the majority of present-day aviation activities at Kirkbride.

Although present-day aviation activity at Kirkbride is now on a much lower key that it was in the war years, John Plaskett and a small but enthusiastic group of private flyers with the support of the field's owners are making a good job of encouraging aviation to return.

CONTRASTING VISITORS TO KIRKBRIDE
– DIGNITY AND IMPUDENCE?

It cannot be denied that Kirkbride is a shadow of its former self when comparing the density of movements of sixty years ago with those of today. However, it has a pleasant, relaxed atmosphere and does not lack variety of visitors, even military, as can be seen from the two pictures on this page.

The Piper Cub shown above is a popular aircraft which private pilots developed from an American spotter plane. This Kirkbride visiting aircraft is a little more interesting than is normal, as part of its registration (JAO) is also three of the letters common to many Cumbrian registered cars. Its livery gives the impression that it might be at home in a Grand Prix, but it is a sobering thought that Formula 1 cars could leave the Cub standing, if you will excuse the expression. The owner who likes flying wouldn't!

The visiting RAF Hercules is one of a formation of three with the futuristic call sign of 'Startrek' while on an exercise. While these visits are not regular, they are also known to have used the other Cumbrian airfields of Carlisle and Walney Island near Barrow in Furness from time to time.

LET-DOWN AND LIFT-OFF OF TWO VERY DIFFERENT TYPES OF AIRCRAFT

The microlight is typical of a number that visit Kirkbride from time to time, seen in the picture letting down. Maybe for Sunday lunch?

The 'lift off' of the preserved Mk 4 Jet Provost G-BWGT trainer would be a very different sight and sound from the microlight in the picture above and only goes to show the versatility and capability of those who run Kirkbride today. As the jet was using runway 28 the photograph was taken looking towards the east, and the mountains in the background must be the northern tip of the Pennines east of Lakeland and beyond the Eden Valley.

Over a period of time the variety of aircraft visiting Kirkbride provide the enthusiast with a feast of contrasts, as do these two twin-engined visitors, both now in the hands of private owners who have lavished much time and money to keep them flying and in pristine condition.

The visiting preserved Percival Pembroke (G-BNPM) pictured above was developed in the late 1950s and '60s as a military transport and for the Navy as the Sea Prince. Percival had become 'Hunting Percival' and stopped production when turbo-prop twins became available, mainly from the American market. This makes the picture below, which was another visiting twin, a Beechcraft Super King Air, typical of the interesting comparisons and the variety of visitors to Kirkbride. In this case there were over forty years between the two designs.

The King Air executive twin is a superb example of progress in development over the last half century to compare with the Pembroke in the picture at the top of the page.

As one of the four remaining active airfields in Lakeland we have given Kirkbride a little extra space. This is not only for its sixty years of existence, but because the sheer variety of traffic it handled in the war years prevents a detailed history which would fill a book on its own.

The non-technical précis given in the way we have on these pages is to indicate the links between the war years and the present day without being boring to those who just want to enjoy what they see.

MORE CONTRASTS SEEN AT KIRKBRIDE IN RECENT TIMES

Not all aircraft to be seen at Kirkbride are as exotic as those shown in photographs on previous pages, but far more typical is the number of privately-owned light aircraft such as the Cessna, probably going to do what most private pilots love to do, flying for pleasure.

A Royal Navy Sea King on the Kirkbride helipad. This aircraft was on a typical Navy 'flag showing' visit. These are always a delight for all as it gives a chance for those who do not live by the sea to see the type of aircraft that are the eyes and ears of the Navy. This particular aircraft was from 849 Squadron with the call sign 'Navy 701'. A cutting in a local paper reports that this visit was a rather special delight for the local schoolchildren

Kirkbride is developing into a very attractive local airfield with great potential. It will be possible to see from the selection of pictures on these pages that there is no attempt to make it a major centre of commercial aviation; there isn't the passenger potential for that anyway. Later on in this book I have made a point or two about the future of aviation in Lakeland and it certainly doesn't include another Heathrow. However, there is enough space for a small 'Air Park' at Kirkbride where private flyers could park their aircraft and hire a car for what could literally be a flying visit to Lakeland!

The aircraft above is a Russian design Yak 52, now registered in the UK and seen here starting up on the apron at Kirkbride.

View along the main runway at Kirkbride with Lakeland Fells on the horizon.

Professional pilots are very blasé when it comes to talking about airfields. They say 7,000 feet of concrete looks much the same the world over. With some of the sophisticated aircraft they fly they haven't time to admire the scenery and this is where pilots with slower light aircraft have them beat. Most are flying 'visual' and when they do land it is true the aerodrome is like others, flat – but once down there is time to enjoy the view, as the sight along the runway at Kirkbride in the photograph above shows.

PARACHUTE CLUB ACTIVITIES AT CARK

The BN Islander aircraft in the picture above is used by the Lancashire Parachute Club, and is seen here waiting on the apron at Cark to take Club members up for a drop.

Below is a parachute group seemingly called the 'Cark Boogie'.

NORTH-WEST PARACHUTE CENTRE AT CARK

Sports are very much to each individual's taste and there would be few to dispute that parachuting is a minority one. Regardless of that, those who do partake have skills which require considerable practice and provide thrills for themselves and often pleasure for onlookers.

There is a well-known adage that 'What goes up must come down'. In the case of parachuting the opposite to this is also true: 'If you must come down, you must first go up!' To do this one of the first requirements is a suitable aeroplane, which could be an Islander such as the one above, as used by the North-West Parachute Centre at Cark.

Exits having been made from the Islander at about 12,000 ft, the aircraft turns away and lands, leaving the airspace above the airfield clear for those making the jump to get into their planned formation.

PARACHUTING AT CARK

Parachuting can take many different forms, of which skydiving is one. It can be a solo jump, tandem jump, or a jump to make many formations on the way down. The pictures on this page are just two examples of these and the way in which members of the North-West Parachute Centre at Cark get their enjoyment at the Lakeland airfield of Cark.

THE FINAL PHASE AND A HAPPY LANDING

After the fun you 'head'(?) for home.

A happy landing 'Batman', and Batwoman! All part of the fun at Cark.

SEARCH AND RESCUE HELICOPTERS

Anywhere around our coastline and in mountainous terrain the need for Search and Rescue facilities has become a necessity. On the coast these are normally controlled by the Coastguard, but inland Police, Fire and Ambulance have to meet the situation with set procedures for operating a tried and tested chain of command in the deployment and use of the available facilities. As far as helicopters are concerned in mountainous areas like Lakeland, the normal authority to call them out is exercised on the judgement of the leader of the Mountain Rescue team.

It was realised by RAF units stationed in Lakeland and Snowdonia that, to reach aircraft which came to grief in the mountains, help would be needed from fit personnel with experience in mountaineering. In fact it took some time before it was officially recognised that there was a very real need for specialised teams to be set up for rescue operations in these areas.

Of course helicopters had not reached the fine pitch of development in those days that would have made them much practical use, but a few Vickers Warwick aircraft were fitted with lifeboats that could be parachuted down to those who ditched in the sea. Some of these were stationed at Great Orton and used on a few operations where it was considered that they could help.

To someone lost or suffering from a broken limb on a wind-swept hilltop the vision of a helicopter approaching must be one of the most beautiful sights in the world.

There can be no apology for using space on helicopters and mountain rescue in a book on Lakeland aviation, for it was less than half a century after the first powered flight by a heavier-than-air aircraft that it was realised that mountains and airplanes did not easily mix. In the Second World War, especially on bases in the Furness area and North Wales, it was realised that to reach crashed aircraft on a mountain was just as important as rescuing an aircrew ditched in the sea.

It is a far cry from the days when a detachment was sent out from Millom or Cark in a Jeep to get as near to a crash and render what aid it could. Now they have teams of volunteers based around mountainous areas equipped with the modern-day Jeep or Land-Rover and radio with the ability to call on helicopters if the team leader decides that help from the air is possible. The large modern aircraft need an extremely high degree of flying skill from the crew as a team in which there are no passengers – each member has a task to do. The pictures on this page give some idea of the complexity of the aircraft which are equipped with just about every conceivable piece of equipment to make possible a rescue and to treat the person or persons rescued with first aid and get them back to safety.

The flight deck of an S61 rescue helicopter is a mind-boggling sight. The cabin is fitted out with every conceivable piece of medical equipment to enable the crew to get a patient back to safety with the greatest speed and comfort.

The skills of the pilots just have to be admired as every situation in which they find themselves is different. Once over the target area, the captain engages the 'auto hover' control which holds the aircraft steady within very tight limits, with Doppler radar. Then the winchman can stand by the door and move the aircraft forwards, backwards or sideways a foot or so by means of a toggle switch situated by the entrance. In this way he has control because the pilot is unable to see what is happening directly below the fuselage.

The present-day Mountain Rescue teams are made up of volunteers, with each team registered as a charity and organising its own situation under the guidance of the The Mountain Rescue Council, who provide support for all the teams in a similar way as the RNLI does for individual lifeboat stations.

A modern-day RAF Search and Rescue helicopter hovering behind the Patterdale Mountain Rescue Team, one of a number of similar teams in Lakeland.

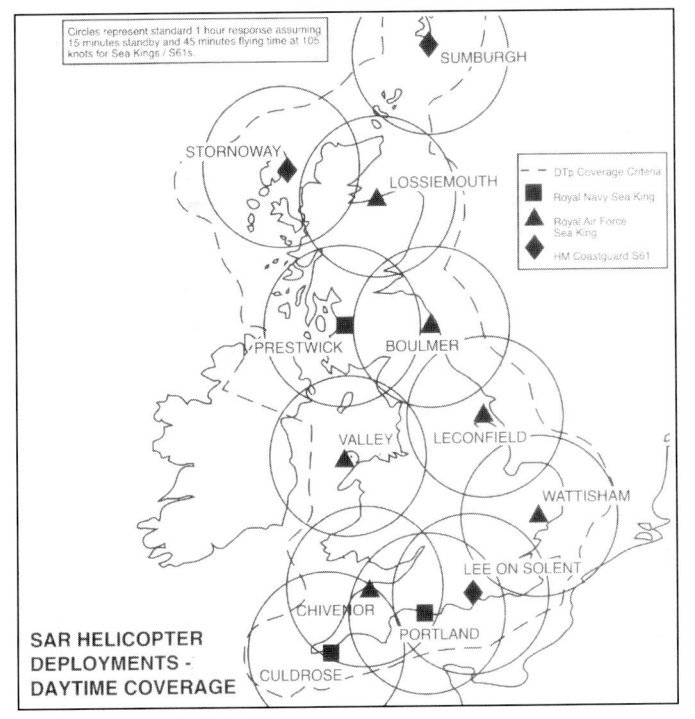

Usually, Police call out a Mountain Rescue team to an incident and the team leader decides if helicopter help is needed. It is the aircraft captain's decision to say if rescue is possible from an aviation point of view.

The map shows the day-time coverage by helicopter bases over the UK. The main base for Lakeland coverage would normally be from RAF Boulmer.

87

JET RANGER AT WORK

It is true to say that most helicopters are 'work horses'; they don't have to be the multi-million pound aircraft such as those used for military and rescue purposes. Smaller ones like the Jet Ranger pictured here have been known to perform dozens of tasks, some usual and others quite unusual. Helicopters have helped to replace a weather cock on a church steeple and have even taken beer to a pub cut off by severe winter weather.

The one shown below was based at Blackpool and was frequently seen at various points in Lakeland.

Oil barrels being dropped into a remote farm in Wasdale.

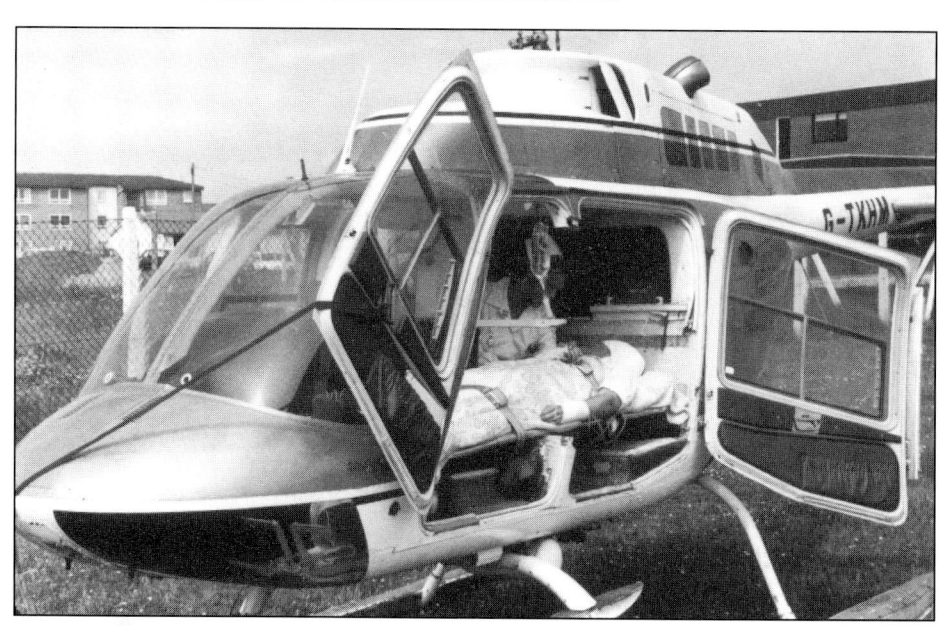

Many a stretcher case has been moved to a hospital where speed and difficulties for other means of transport make the helicopter essential.

THE START OF A HOT AIR BALLOON FLIGHT

A quiet, calm morning, the promise of a gentle breeze from the opposite direction to the way you would like to go, plenty of propane and after a comfortable night, off you go!

Needless to say, it would be OK if it was always like that, and you might do it every day. However, the increasingly popular aviation activity is very satisfying in Lakeland, as the following pictures will show.

OVER THE FELLS

Take off shortly after dawn from a site near Windermere, let the air take you over the superb scenery of snow-capped Skiddaw, past Keswick to an equally pleasant site at the Ullswater Hotel. That's good navigation!

OTHER LAKELAND BALLOON FLIGHTS

All balloon trips in Lakeland are spectacular, some are serene, some a little rough, but all are memorable. The trip on the previous page was spectacular, and the one above was memorable as the fell (top left) is Scafell Pike – at 3,200 feet, the highest peak in England.

Top right is over Honister Pass which at this point in the flight was dictating that a landing was needed. Some landings are smooth, some rough, and as can be seen below this one could have been rough. However, all landings from which you can walk away are good ones. True, even in Lakeland where some terrain is very rough!

INTO THE 21ST CENTURY

As we turn into the twenty-first century it behoves us well to look at the past and consider the future. The past falls logically into three distinct parts. The first was roughly from 1900 to the outbreak of the Second World War when the entrepreneurs were as keen as anybody to join in with this new phase in history called flying. The possibility that manned flight should be developed and that the Lakeland area might be left behind was not even considered.

The development of the area as a holiday centre caught on, with the impetus given to it by the railways and the development of road transport. Those who could afford a holiday at all went to the fleshpots of Morecambe or Blackpool and left the peace and beauty of the Lakes to those who preferred it to sticks of rock and candy floss. The exception was Carlisle which did set up the second airport in the country to be licensed as a municipal airport. This gave it some status in the world of aviation, but its geographical hinterland and being in what by other standards was the middle of a sparsely populated area prevented it from developing commercially.

Aviation came north with the onset of the Second World War which transformed the area around the Lakes from an aeronautical desert to one where flying was as intensive as anywhere else in Great Britain. This mushroom growth was explained by the threat of war and the remoteness from the parts of the country which fully expected to be deluged by bombing as soon as war was declared. This seemed to be a good idea at the time. In fact it was, and served the purpose very well in spite of the inhibiting factors which did and still do prevent Cumbria, as it now is, from developing the use of aviation as has happened in most of the rest of the country.

The end of the war saw the rapid run-down and complete closure of most of the sixteen airfields which were built in the three years between 1939 and 1942. Today at the beginning of a new century we are left with four active sites still being operated to a greater or lesser extent. Two of these are in the Furness area, one being a private airfield operated by the shipbuilding interests at Barrow and the other operated by a parachute club. Of the two in the north, one is a private unlicensed airfield but very usable at the pilots' own risk. The fourth one is the old RAF field, Crosby on Eden, which was bought by the Carlisle City Council to replace the old site at Kingston which could not handle modern aircraft.

It has to be said that Carlisle Airport, as it is now known, has been a disappointment and not developed commercially as was hoped. It is now a small regional airport with enough facilities to cater for such demands that are made on it. Some scheduled routes were tried in an effort to link the City Airport with other developing areas but unfortunately modern development overtook them and these projects were all short lived.

From the outsider's point of view it is worth looking at the reasons for this because they in turn will give positive pointers to the way ahead.

Without being cynical, there are three main reasons for Carlisle Airport not growing as many others have done.

One is its geographical position. The hinterland has little supporting industry now, with the decline in the use of coal and other natural resources, and is predominately rural, thinly populated with a holiday trade that is highly seasonal. In other words 'the numbers game' is against it.

Secondly, fifty miles away is a major international and regional airport at Newcastle with a good industrial hinterland to make that airport a viable proposition.

Thirdly, Lakeland is not ideal for aviation, with mountains on three sides as well as in the centre, which means that modern alternative transport is cheaper and more convenient.

These facts do not mean that Carlisle's airport should be closed, because it still can, and does, serve a useful purpose. It only means that the services and facilities have to be restricted to the potential income. There is some summer charter traffic and local industries can and do take advantage of it. Private flying and training are two other activities which give a small but useful income and there is also room to provide facilities for cargo traffic, not to mention that it can be vital in emergencies where diversions are forced upon flights from other destinations. Efforts are being made to develop use along these lines and there is still hope that future development will be able to turn what is already *in situ* to good use.

Looking at Lakeland in the terms we have set for ourselves in this book, we now should turn to the future. To coin a phrase or two, 'we have the technology' to turn 'pie in the sky' into 'planes in the sky'. The questions are, do we need to and do we want to? The answer to the first part of the question is probably, No. However, to the second question the answer, with reservations, is Yes.

In a limited way the indications of how aviation is likely to develop in Lakeland is given on these pages. For instance, helicopters are used for two very different purposes: firstly in a vital rôle in mountain rescue and secondly giving access for those who can afford it, or have need, to hotels, conferences or business meetings where time is limited and costs are of secondary importance.

The use of aviation for recreation or sport can be seen in its application to such activities as hot air ballooning, hang gliding and parascending, and even parachuting, which do little to desecrate the area but give some great pleasure.

We are told that military training involving flying very noisy and supersonic aircraft a couple of hundred feet above our heads and below the peaks, which we have come to 'enjoy' in peacetime, is vital to the nation. Unfortunately there can be few who will argue with the reason for this, but we all say 'not in our backyard' to it.

There were over thirty airships in service and flying regularly at the beginning of the century, with another dozen or so on order. There is a project for a real giant to carry 160 tonnes of freight which is expected to be flying in the year 2001. This will be a very large 'pie in the sky' indeed, but there are also a number with more modest capacities already on order and being built as fifty-two seaters. It needs not too much stretch of the imagination to see how an airship of this sort of capacity could operate a 'park and ride shuttle' from, say, Kendal or Penrith to the very heart of the Lakes. It would be quiet, safe and need little in the way of ground facilities.

Outside London, the Lake District National Park attracts more tourists than any other part of the UK, and aviation as it has been mainly used up to now has not had the possibility of exploiting this to any great degree. However, with modern technology, materials and non-inflammable helium gas, the airship in its new form does have a really great potential and would offer a new and very attractive way to travel to the area. Aviation has a real potential in Lakeland.

The above is not all 'pie in the sky' because the five-seat AT10s and larger are flying now.

BIBLIOGRAPHY

Title	Author	Publisher	Date
Pooley's Flight Guide (UK & Ireland) 1995	Robert Pooley	Pooley's Flight Guides	1995
Action Stations No. 3 Wales & The North-West	David J. Smith	PSL	1984
British Airports	Leo Marriot	Ian Allan Ltd	1993
The Short Sunderland	Chas Bowyer	Aston Publications	1989
Air To Ground	Ken Davies	Ian Allan Ltd	1995
Aircraft of the Royal Air Force since 1918	Owen Thetford	Putnam	1995
Short Aircraft since 1900	C. H. Barnes	Putnam	1982
The Great Age of Steam on Windermere	George H. Pattinson	Windermere Nautical Trust	1981
Windermere Steamboat Museum	A Guide	Museum Trust	1997
Carlisle Airport. A History of Crosby on Eden Airfield 1914-91	Paul Wiggins	Solway Aviation Society	1991
British Commercial Aircraft	Paul Ellis	Janes Publishing Co.	1980
Airports UK	Peter Crook	Unknown	c.1995
History of the RAF	Chas Bowyer	Bison Books Ltd	1994
Ref. to OS Maps 85, 86, 89, 90, 91 (OS Landranger Series)		Ordnance Survey	

ACKNOWLEDGEMENTS

Before anything else is said I need to point out that when selecting from such a vast number of sources it is not possible to acknowledge every illustration actually used in this book. The fact is that most are from my own collection which has been accumulated over nearly half a century in my scrap books and collection of cuttings. I have seen quite a few, some even of my own, with differing credits given by different publishers.

It has not always been possible to trace the original source, even if it is still available, and where this is so the best available has had to be used. Where there is some doubt and such organisations as museums are quoted by some publishers and not others, the least I can say is, if they are the originators, 'Thank you'. I have also received considerable help from the Imperial War Museum, the RAF Museum and a number of other collections.

The following receive my special thanks for the loan or donation of illustrations, paper cuttings and other items without which this book would not have been possible:

John Plaskett, co-ordinator at Kirkbride, for the wealth of information he gladly supplied;

David Barnes of Preston who had the navigational skills on his own safari to take pictures of a number of old sites which look very like the fields next to them half a century later;

Mr Newby Tate of Brampton who has been a mine of information and obtained pictures from his many local contacts, as well as his own long and practical connections with aviation;

Robbie Mansfield of High Adventure Balloon Flights for his superb pictures of the gentle art (sometimes) of hot air ballooning over the Lake District;

Neil Thexton of Lancaster for the fascinating pictures of the last visit of a flying boat to Windermere;

the Windermere Steamboat Museum for the pictures of the experimental glider seaplane;

the Press Officer of VSEL for pictures of the private corporate aircraft operated from Barrow in Furness;

and the Cumbria County Librarians at Barrow in Furness, Kendal and Carlisle, who have given me their unstinting help in my research efforts.

Lastly, but certainly not least, my wife Barbara, who is spell checker and proof reader extraordinaire and puts up with my absence at the keyboard for hours on end.